THE

WORD

AN EVANGELISTIC MANIFESTO

MIKE HILSON & CURTIS HUNNICUTT

CONTENTS

ABOUT THIS BOOK

As we serve today in multiple roles within the Body of Christ, we seemingly serve in a world that has gone mad. Society seems to be coming apart, and the church has exited the debate. Churches that once led the call for repentance, holiness, justice, grace, and peace are now either silent or adhering to a particular political brand. Even churches that are growing seem to be attempting to attract people to a quality show than a loving Savior. It seems that in our well-meaning pursuit of an accepting and loving Christian culture and our open-minded pursuit of social justice, we have hidden the name of our Savior within the slogan of our current chosen cause.

What is going on?

In this book, we tackle the weakness that has invaded the Church in North America. In doing this, we look at philosophies and values that have entered the thinking of church leaders and congregants. We delve into the ever-changing definitions of terms and understanding of purpose within ministry and churches. We do all of this from a historical, philosophical, theological, and evangelistic vantage point.

To regain our voice as followers of Jesus, we *must* speak the right message and live out the right mission. Our words and our actions must line up. We no longer have the luxury of saying whatever we want and assuming our words have authority because there is a *Rev.* in front of our name or because we speak on behalf of a historical congregation. Today, the words we speak must be carefully chosen and Christ-centered.

Let's be clear. Sin is the problem.

Grace is the answer.

Jesus died to be our source of grace.

But if we remain on our current trajectory, how will our culture ever hear about Jesus? How will they ever hear about *grace* if we don't tell them? How will we effectively communicate biblical Truth again?

Truth is not new, but it is often forgotten and buried beneath the very institutions designed to showcase it.

People need the Jesus we preach.

Let's talk about Him again!

"How, then, can they call on the one they have not believed in? And how can they believe in the one of whom they have not heard? And how can they hear without someone preaching to them? And how can anyone preach unless they are sent? As it is written: 'How beautiful are the feet of those who bring good news!'"

—Romans 10:14-15

Pastor Mike Hilson
Pastor Curtis Hunnicutt

PART

HOW DID WE GET HERE?

> **❝** The proportion of Christians in America is declining, a clear trend that is likely to continue—especially because Gen Z (who are not reflected in this study as a separate group) self-identifies as atheist at twice the rate of US adults overall (13% vs. 7%). Barna tracking data since 1996 shows a sharp rise in those identifying as atheist, agnostic or "none"/no faith, alongside a nearly matching decline in "born again" Christians.[1]

—Barna, *Reviving Evangelism*

1

THE DYING ART

Evangelism is a dying art.

But you will receive power when the Holy Spirit comes on you; and you will be my witnesses in Jerusalem, and in all Judea and Samaria, and to the ends of the earth.

—Acts 1:8

Evangelism | "The winning or revival of personal commitments to Christ."[1]

It was the summer between high school and college. I (Mike) had just arrived at my summer job on a construction site run by my stepdad. It was just another Monday working as the lowest ranking flunky on the construction crew. But that particular day was different. It was different for two reasons.

One of those reasons was I had spent every night of the week prior at a "Go Tell" crusade preached by an evangelist named Freddie Gage. At the time, he was one of many evangelists who traveled around the country holding week-long evangelistic crusades designed to bring those who did not know Jesus as their Savior to the point of choosing to become a Jesus follower. He was working to see a "revival of personal commitments to Christ."[2]

The entire week, I listened intently as Freddie Gage implored each of us to "Go Tell" everyone we knew about

Jesus, the One who wanted to be the Savior of every person in the world. I thought about my co-workers on the construction site, but they didn't seem like the right candidate for my Good News. That entire week passed, and I didn't "Go Tell."

That day was also different because two of our co-workers didn't show for work. They were best friends around the same age who oddly enough married a mother and daughter. Yeah, it was weird, but you know. When I asked my stepdad why they weren't there, he informed me that Ricky had not come home over the weekend, and they were looking for him. So, like any good Christian kid, I prayed for him. The next day, my stepdad took me aside and gave me some of the worst news I had ever heard. He said, "Michael, they found Ricky. Somebody murdered him and dumped his body in the abandoned antique shop." It was one of those moments when the entire world begins to fade a bit around you, and you feel trapped in the closing darkness of one simple, horrible truth. I failed Ricky! I didn't "Go Tell" him!

I swore to myself in the grief of that day that I would not let that happen to me again. I would tell people every chance I had about Jesus and His love for them. I would commit myself to always "Go Tell." Now, I cannot say that I have 100 percent lived up to that promise, but that is another story for another day.

This deep-seated desire to reach those who have not yet chosen to become followers of Jesus was real and passionately ingrained in my soul that day, and honestly, it still is. That passion is known by its biblical word, *evangelism.*

There is a difference between then and now. Then, in 1985, my passion was in good company. There were programs for evangelism, conferences for evangelism, and discipleship groups to train churchgoers in evangelism. Almost every Saturday, someone would show up at the door of your home and attempt to share the Good News of Jesus with you and invite you to their church. Almost every Sunday, there would be an altar call at church where the pastor called those who had not yet prayed the *sinner's prayer* to come forward and receive forgiveness in Jesus' name. Evangelism was everywhere.

Things have changed.

According to research done by the Barna Group: "A majority of practicing Christians do not consistently support evangelism, and 47 percent of Millennial Christians believe it is flat-out wrong to evangelize."[3] In another study led by Barna Group's president, David Kinnaman, it was discovered that "a startling six in 10 Americans believe that any 'attempt to convert others' to one's own faith is 'extreme.' More than eight out of 10 atheists, agnostics and nones say so! To be clear: A majority of US adults, and the vast majority of non-religious adults (83%), believe that evangelism is religiously extreme."[4]

This lack of evangelistic interest follows on the heels of almost two centuries of anti-religious thought from groups that today are fairly dominant within the academic, media, and political world. Forty years ago, it would have been unthinkable that the teachings of Karl Marx would be preeminent among the most educated and influential people in our society. Yet, today, this seems to be the case. The rejection of God and religion, which is central to Marxism, is now considered the only absolute truth allowed in a culture that no longer accepts the existence of absolute truth. The problem is that even after almost 200 years of attempts, the goal that this thinking promised has yet to be achieved. Leon Trotsky, one of the founders of Soviet/Russian Communism, made the expectations of atheistic Communism and Marxist thought clear: "Man will make it his purpose to master his own feelings, to raise his instincts to the heights of consciousness, to make them transparent, to extend the wires of his will into hidden recesses, and thereby to raise himself to a new plane, to create a higher social biologic type, or, if you please, a superman."[5]

In the wake of the destruction of what we now know of as the history of Russian Communism, as well as Communist/Marxist attempts elsewhere, the hope of a biological "superman" has been crushed beneath the reality of the brokenness of the real human. While Marxism promised to usher in the utopia of humankind without the evil of greed and private property, or the *opiate* of God and religion, it instead seemed to have proved the ancient Christian theology of original sin. Communist leaders, who claimed to be leading people into a utopian reality through reason and science, killed more of their own people than every war in human history combined. Joseph Stalin and Mao Tse-tung killed between 70 and 100 million of their own citizens during times of *peace*.[6]

So much for Trotsky's *superman.*

Where has all of this left us?

> Godless philosophies have left us wounded, while godlessness itself has left us empty.

Within my own tribe (Wesleyans), these thoughts have recently displayed themselves. We have sat together in multiple rooms and asked ourselves why our attendance and growth have been in decline for a few years now. While most mainline denominations have experienced a steady decline over the last 40 years, Wesleyans have reversed that trend. The denomination saw modest growth year after year for most of the time between the 1970s through the early 2000s. "In 1970 some 103,534 people attended worship at Wesleyan churches on an average Sunday."[7] By 2018, attendance at Wesleyan churches on an average Sunday had reached 235,100. As wonderful as that number sounds, it represents a two percent decline compared to the 2017 number, which set a downward trend.[8] It seems that we have begun to see the same decline as our mainline cousins have experienced.

Why?

A careful look at the publications and proclamations of the denomination will reveal a shift in terminology. In the past, we spoke strongly and often about evangelism and holiness, but today, we rarely hear these words. Today, we talk about other goals. These goals are sincere. They are true to our heritage as Wesleyans, and they are noble causes. They include such things as diversity, social justice, and political activism. These things were part of our DNA from the very inception of our movement. The Wesleyan Methodist Connection (the founding body that became The Wesleyan Church in 1968) was founded as a protest against the unwillingness of the larger United Methodist Church to take a stand against slavery.

66 On November 8, 1842, three prominent Methodist abolitionists—Orange Scott, LaRoy Sunderland, and Jotham Horton—announced that they were withdrawing from the denomination. Within weeks they were joined by two others, Luther Lee and Lucius Matlack. They had come to believe, Scott said, that it would be a sin for them to remain in a church

that seemed so intent on betraying its anti slavery heritage.[9]

This activist history is something of which we are very proud. However, it must be practiced and understood within the context of the primary call of the Church to spread the Good News of Jesus to anyone and everyone that will listen. Those brave leaders fought for the freedom and dignity of every human being, but they did so in the name of the God who created them and the Jesus who saved them.

To say it another way, a focus on evangelism can and, I believe most often, will lead to taking a stand for justice for all people because all people are created in the image of God. However, starting with a stand for social justice does not lead to evangelism. Over and over again in every culture, people have fought for justice without finding spiritual freedom.

> Therefore, the declining growth and influence of any denomination that trades its central focus of evangelism to social issues should not come as a surprise.

In this book, we will focus on the final call of Christ to all of us as His Church. As He was about to leave this earth after His resurrection, Jesus said to His disciples, "But you will receive power when the Holy Spirit comes on you; and you will be my witnesses in Jerusalem, and in all Judea and Samaria, and to the ends of the earth" (Acts 1:8). The power of the Holy Spirit was given in Acts, chapter 2, for the purpose of being witnesses to the death, burial, resurrection, and forgiving power of Jesus, and the transforming power of the Holy Spirit.

This is where our work must begin.

To start anywhere else would result in failure.

2

OAK TREES & CRABGRASS

Movements naturally become institutions. But can an institution become a movement?

When I fed them, they were satisfied; when they were satisfied, they became proud; then they forgot me.

—Hosea 13:6

Institution | "An established organization or corporation (as a college or university) especially of a public character."[1]

Movement | "The act or process of moving; especially : change of place or position or posture; a tactical or strategic shifting of a military unit; a series of organized activities working toward an objective."[2]

His name was Rev. H. W. Hawkins. I (Mike) had just started work as the pastor of Sandy Ridge Wesleyan Church in Hickory, North Carolina. As I was going through the desk to set myself up in this new world I had just entered, I found a pictorial directory of what was called the Wesleyan Methodist Church of North Carolina. In this directory, I found the church I had grown up in, multiple churches where Tina and I had served, and the church where I had just become the pastor. As I thumbed through the entries, I noticed a couple of names repeated over and over again as the founders of different churches. Hawkins' name appeared time after time as the founding pastor of churches all across the area.

Rev. Hawkins, it seemed, had a habit of moving into a town and holding a series of events that attracted people. He communicated the Good News of Jesus in such a way that people became followers of Jesus. He would then plant a church in which they would work and grow together in the power of the Holy Spirit. According to the North Carolina District Centennial published in 1979, Rev. Roy S. Nicholson said, "His [Rev. Hawkins] labors in North Carolina, South Carolina, Georgia, Tennessee, Virginia and New Jersey resulted in the organization of 35 Wesleyan churches."[3] As I began to realize all the churches Rev. Hawkins had planted, the people he had reached, and the lives that were transformed as a result of his work, I made a decision. That's what I want to do! From that moment, my passion for starting churches and ministries took hold. From that moment forward, I made a vow to myself that I would spend my life attempting to launch a movement of evangelism followed by church planting that would change lives and, ultimately, change culture. At the time, it seemed like an impossible goal for a 24-year old rookie preacher.

That internal drive to somehow launch a movement of life-changing churches and Christians led me to spend the last 30 years obsessing over other movements that have, for good or bad, changed the culture in which we live. History is filled with stories of people who have launched movements that somehow attracted large crowds. Some have built churches, denominations, businesses, political parties, and even cities and nations. All were unique as an expression of combined passion and skill, and yet each had a singular trait that set them apart.

A truly powerful movement requires a truly powerful vision.

Movements can always trace back to an overwhelming passion for an overarching vision of how the world should be, which exists in an individual or a small group of individuals. Virtually everyone has an idea of how the world should be better or different. However, only a few have the capacity and passion to communicate a vision with arguments so compelling that thousands or even millions of people are won over. Here are a few examples of that.

A VISION OF FREEDOM

On the North American continent, a group of leaders had a truly powerful vision for a nation that would be "of the people, by the people, for the people," as is stated in Abraham Lincoln's Gettysburg Address.[4] The founders of the United States of America envisioned a nation founded on the freedom of all people to pursue their own version of "Life, Liberty and the pursuit of Happiness," as is stated in the Declaration of Independence (US 1776). This powerful vision drove the founders and future defenders of this nation to work, fight, and even die for these freedoms so that their vision could become a reality.

A VISION OF EQUALITY

Karl Marx, the 19th-century German philosopher, dreamed of a world where classism would be eradicated and replaced instead with an equal and just system of wealth and social management. His powerful vision, known as socialism, became the driving force behind many governmental structures and social experiments throughout the next 200 years.

A VISION OF CONTROL

Joseph Stalin, Mao Tse-tung, and others took Marx's vision of equality and layered onto it a vision of control. Seeing that socialism was not progressing rapidly enough for them toward the promised inevitable communist state, they implemented regimes of strict control, violence, and even oppression. They did this to achieve their version of a Marxist vision of equality amongst their nation and people.

A VISION OF REDEMPTION

And then there is Jesus. At first glance, one might not see Jesus in the same category of leader. The founders of the USA, socialist thought, the USSR, and the People's Republic of China would seem to be on a higher scale than the simple Jewish rabbi who was unjustly murdered by angry Jewish crowds and a willing, if not hesitant, Roman governor. However, Jesus' vision of a world redeemed by one perfect sacrifice was so powerful and profound that it predates and postdates all political and thought leaders previously mentioned, as well as those not mentioned. His vision of redemption supersedes and pervades their visions of freedom, equality, and control.

Each of these visions faced one similar challenge: Institutionalization.

Movements are defined by their movement.

I know that seems simplistic, but it is actually important. A movement that is no longer in motion cannot, in reality, be called a movement. Here is a typical life cycle of a movement:

Sincere beginnings lead to passionate proclamations, which will lead to powerful acceptance, which leads to widespread control, which ultimately leads to institutionalization. Once institutionalized, the motion of the movement becomes constricted and grinds to a halt.

Institutionalization is a natural outcome of powerful movements, not because people want to slow the movement down. On the contrary, the people who begin the institutionalization of a movement are the ones who are most passionate and committed to the movement itself. Their goal is to define the movement and defend it. They keep it from losing its way in the fog of intense growth and influence or hijacked by people who do not belong. They define who should be part of the movement, who should lead the movement, who should follow the movement, and what direction the movement should head. Conversely, they define the negative of all of these. They define who cannot belong, lead, follow, or direct the movement. Once this work is complete, the movement is safe from being corrupted by those who do not understand. It is safe from those who might attempt to change, redefine, or redirect the passion and power of the movement. But there is an unintentional outcome of this intentional protection: The loss of movement. Consider the following outcomes.

AN INSTITUTIONALIZED VISION OF FREEDOM

Somehow in their quest for freedom, the founders of the United States forgot their own words in the Declaration of Independence. "We hold these truths to be self-evident, that all men are created equal, that they are endowed by their Creator with certain unalienable Rights, that among these are Life, Liberty and the pursuit of Happiness" (US 1776). As the defenders of this new movement began to institutionalize the passions and dreams of this new nation, they decided that those who could lead would only be white males. While this was a fairly normal European pattern of thought for the day, it did not reflect the words they had just penned, signed, and risked their lives to make real. Therefore, the institutionalization of their declaration hindered the continued movement of their stated goals. This hindrance still haunts the U.S. today.

AN INSTITUTIONALIZED VISION OF EQUALITY

Karl Marx and his philosophy known as Marxism have seen myriad iterations of institutionalization. These iterations have worked or failed, to varying degrees of prosperity and terror, but they all have one thing in common. The ideal of equality must be governed by some institutionalized system of control. In the best cases, the institution is cumbersome and laborious, and often painfully slow. But in the worst cases, this institutionalization is deadly on a scale never seen before in human history.

AN INSTITUTIONALIZED VISION OF CONTROL

The greatest horrors of institutional socialism have come at the hands of leaders like Stalin and Mao. While there are more examples of the horrific way socialism/communism was institutionalized, these two outdid all the others. In an effort to crush all systems of class, except the powerful one they lived in, these two leaders killed more people than all wars in human history combined.

Some estimates place Mao's murderous outcomes at 70 million Chinese,[5] and some place Stalin as high as 20 million citizens of the USSR.[6] Keep in mind, foreign, hostile power did not kill these people. Their own leader and their own government killed them.

AN INSTITUTIONALIZED VISION OF REDEMPTION

Unfortunately, this same process happens in Christianity. The institution of the Church has attempted for more than 2,000 years to protect Christianity from heresy and confusion. We have done the great and noble work of defining Christian theology and doctrine. We have defended the faith from attacks coming from literally every conceivable people group and angle. The institution of the Christian Church is impressive in human history, simply for its ability to survive, even thrive, throughout persecutions, wars, political upheaval, economic crisis, famine, disease, and internal failures. Throughout all of this, the Church has continued to stand and spread the Word of Jesus.

But the movement has slowed.

In fact, in the long-standing strongholds of Christianity, the movement has stopped, and decline has taken hold. Europe, which was once the global center of Christian thinking and mission, has seen such a significant decline in practicing Christians that the Pew

Research Center wrote the following: "Western Europe, where Protestant Christianity originated and Catholicism has been based for most of its history, has become one of the world's most secular regions."[7] This secularization of Europe's population can be attributed to many factors. One of those factors, the intense institutionalization of the Church in Europe, cannot be ignored. Whether speaking of Catholicism or Protestantism, the deeply rooted desire of Christian leaders to maintain and protect the providential tenets of the Christian faith has worked to exclude vast portions of surrounding populations. What began as a sincere attempt to protect and defend Truth has unfortunately turned into a restrictive, exclusive gateway to the Almighty. Worse yet, when it occurs, the people who call themselves Christians seem unconcerned that they have disenfranchised so many from the Hope given for everyone.

When the goal of the Church becomes purity, the passion of the Church is turned inward. This turning inward has happened in so many different ways that it is impossible to track them all in any readable length of study. Let's consider two.

The purity demanded by the Church can take the form of legalism. This demands that everyone who wishes for salvation follow a strict set of rules and regulations in order to earn a place among the redeemed. Each unique group of legalists establishes its rules by attempting to have others live as they do. Dress this way, talk this way, worship this way. This practice often leads to an angry, closed-off group of self-righteous holy rollers who honestly no longer care about those who have not yet discovered Jesus. The only concern they have is seeing those in the group conform to the norms of the group. In this setting, evangelism can happen only when it is done in conformity. Therefore, the theology boils down to the following: Get right so you can get Jesus.

On the other hand, this demand for purity can take the form of a passionate pursuit of social justice that seems incapable of viewing people, society, or the Bible from any vantage point other than oppression and power. In this scenario, the Church becomes filled with self-righteous activists demanding that everyone show the social cues of acceptance and tolerance before possibly being redeemed. Again, this leads to an almost complete lack of concern for anyone outside of that thought pattern who has yet to find Christ. This theology tends to boil down to the following: Save society to save your own soul.

This kind of institutionalization, legalistic bent or activist bent, is absolute poison for the true spread of Christianity. Jesus takes us as we are: broken, angry, hateful, sad, clueless, dirty, sinful people who can be saved by His sacrifice and then made new by the power of the Holy Spirit.

All this begs a big question.

Can a movement that has become an institution become a movement again?

Our desired answer to this question is an emphatic YES! As part of a denominational tribe that we love and have served in for many years, we share the desire with so many others to see the institution we serve return to the movement it once was. We desire a Church that is "transforming lives, churches and communities through the hope and holiness of Jesus Christ."[8] In many ways, this is exactly what is going on. The problem is that the institution, though it is well-meaning, well-designed, and well-led, hinders the flexibility required of the movement. Therefore, we fear that the answer to this one big question is NO . . . unless . . . the evangelist willingly submits to the structure of the institution while the institution allows for the chaotic work of the evangelist.

This balance of mutual voluntary submission will not be easy. Institutions are not designed for flexibility or mobility. They are designed to settle in and defend. Likewise, a movement is not designed to stay contained within walls. It is more like an invading army. A walled city would be an institution securely sitting behind its walls, while a movement would be the invading army that threatens those very walls or at least insists on escaping them. Both are significant. Both are important. Both have their place in shaping and developing a culture and a society, but they are profoundly different things.

Christian institutions are like walled cities. They guard and protect the very core of our doctrines, theologies, and practices. They are important and must be understood and valued for the vital role they play.

Evangelistic movements are more like an invading army. They seek to infiltrate communities and groups of people with the hope of Christ and the power of the Holy Spirit. They get messy and tend to frustrate, even frighten, their brothers and sisters behind the walls of institutions. But without the new converts evangelists win, the institutions have no hope of a future.

The degree to which the difference between institutionalization and evangelization is realized will depend largely on the nature of the institution in question. Here are some examples.

A MYOPIC INSTITUTION

Some institutions are so singularly focused that there seems to be no need for greater flexibility or freedom to accomplish the mission or achieve motion. A myopic institution never senses a need for reform or change. Since this group only attracts people who wish to be part of a group that does the one thing they do, there is no sense of restriction or frustration. Through my years in ministry, I have marveled at leaders who claim, "everyone in our church is in a small group," or "everyone in our church is in a prayer ministry," or even, "everyone in our church is a true worshipper." I have struggled with whether to call these leaders liars or delusional. Then one day, one leader said the following: "We simply tell people when they come the first time that we are a church that insists on everyone being in a small group. So if that is not OK with you, then find another church." Now it makes sense. Since that is all they do, then that is all they attract. The restrictions of the institution define the people being reached leaving no sense of any need for change. Furthermore, other leaders who value what they have institutionalized will celebrate them and at the next conference, that leader will be a guest speaker for (insert your favorite ministry here).

As an evangelistic strategy, this is limiting.

A DIVERSE INSTITUTION

Most institutions are not so singularly focused. Most wrestle with varying degrees of definitions of words like holiness, salvation, justice, grace, and the like. Within most denominations, there are people on the fringes of every iteration possible of what it means to be a committed follower of Christ. These fringe followers will blend in with a whole lot of people who are just coming because they like the ministries, the sermons, the music, or whatever they have found in this one particular church. They live oblivious to the institution of which that church is a part. In these more diverse institutions, restrictions are most sharply felt by those who live on the fringes causing friction between deeply committed individuals who have opposing core values.

THE ANATOMY OF INSTITUTIONS & MOVEMENTS

The real challenge exists in the simple anatomy of institutions and movements. They are just not the same animal! While institutions desire to build cities and protect them with thick walls, movements desire to mount horses and take new lands. While institutions yearn for purity in thought and action, movements yearn for the messiness of untrained newbies. While institutions demand structure, movements defy structure. Let me illustrate it this way.

OAK TREES

Institutions are like oak trees. They take a long time to develop. They establish deep roots in the theological and doctrinal foundations to which they hold dear. They have the capacity to grow to great heights and give cover to great societal spaces. They are large, strong, and impressive. This is no dig on the institution of the Church. As stated earlier in this chapter, the survival of the Church over the past 2,000 years is historically impressive, and the institution of the Church has had much to do with that glorious and miraculous story. However, oak trees are very slow growing and not very helpful to anything that wishes to grow under them. They demand most of the nutrients in the soil surrounding them, and they take most of the sunlight that falls on them, leaving anything wishing to grow under them malnourished and sun-deprived.

CRABGRASS

Movements are more like crabgrass. They tend not to grow very tall or be very impressive to the untrained eye. But they spread like wildfire! A simple Google search for *crabgrass* will prove the strength and resilience of this simple little plant, as the main topic is *how to kill crabgrass.*

Often, the Church is necessarily an institution, an oak tree, while evangelism is necessarily a movement, crabgrass. While it is possible for the movement of evangelism to occur within the structure of the institution of a given denomination, it is simply one of many competing priorities. The institution of the Church must champion all of the following: evangelism, discipleship, worship, theology, doctrine, justice, legal issues, property issues, financial issues, leadership training, leadership failure, and the list can go on and on. These are all important priorities that must be recognized and dealt with inside of the institution of the Church. Over time, these competing priorities begin to push and pull against one another at sometimes alarming rates. If something does not rise to the top as the main thing that we can keep as the main thing, the institution itself will eventually begin to fray and come apart.

We are convinced that evangelism, the reaching of those who have not yet become followers of Christ, is the main thing that we must keep as the main thing. This is not to diminish the other priorities mentioned as well as the ones not mentioned. Instead, it is the natural prioritization of those priorities that must happen intentionally within the institution of the Church. As you react for or against the primacy of evangelism, keep in mind the following: If there are no new believers, then eventually those who disciple have no one to disciple, the worshippers have no one to lead in worship, the preachers have no one to preach to, the justice warriors have no one to march alongside them, and the treasurers have no generosity to manage. All of these priorities and more are incredibly important. None can be deleted from the Body of Christ without creating a wretched and disfigured body. However, none of them can accomplish their mission without beginning at the point of evangelizing new people to the grace of Christ.

When we make evangelism the first thing, and we keep the first thing first, all the rest will follow in the guidance and power of the Holy Spirit!

3

THE WORTH OF THE ONE

66

When I was younger, my greatest fear in ministry was becoming a liberal. As I get older, my greatest fear in ministry is failing to show grace.

—Mike Hilson

The end of all things is near. Therefore be alert and of sober mind so that you may pray. Above all, love each other deeply, because love covers over a multitude of sins.

—1 Peter 4:7-8

Individualism | "A doctrine that the interests of the individual are or ought to be ethically paramount; the conception that all values, rights, and duties originate in individuals; a theory maintaining the political and economic independence of the individual and stressing individual initiative, action, and interests."[1]

Collectivism | "A political or economic theory advocating collective control especially over production and distribution or a system marked by such control."[2]

66 After a season of prayer, Brother
Crooks arose, his cheeks pale as marble
. . . "I will go," he said. "Sustained by
your prayers, and in the name of my
Savior, I will go to North Carolina."[3]

—Robert Black and Keith Drury,
The Story of The Wesleyan Church

Never had it seemed so dangerous to go to North
Carolina. The state that I (Mike) grew up in and
felt such a deep, personal connection to had a much
darker past than I understood as a child. Growing up in
rural North Carolina and attending Wesleyan churches
my entire life, I never understood the actual history. The
above quote is from Rev. Adam Crooks. He was called to
ministry through an abolitionist minister in Leesville,
Ohio. After receiving his training in 1843, he accepted
the most unlikely of calls. It seemed that his mentor had
preached an anti-slavery sermon in a Presbyterian church
in Cincinnati that had caught the attention, through
printed pamphlets, of a group of abolitionists in North
Carolina. "He delivered a powerful antislavery address,
so powerful that Quaker abolitionists printed and
distributed two thousand copies of it. One of the copies
of the speech, which was entitled 'Love Worketh No Ill to
His Neighbor' (see Rom. 13:10 KJV), [these pamphlets]

came to the attention of a Methodist congregation in North Carolina" (TWC, 46-47). When the pastor of the Methodist church rejected the content of the pamphlet, a group from the congregation decided to launch a new Wesleyan Methodist Church. They banded together and sent word to the Wesleyans in Ohio that they needed a Pastor.

Adam Crooks said yes.

That choice changed everything in his life. The church he founded, Freedom's Hill Wesleyan Methodist Church in Snow Camp, North Carolina in 1847, became a focal point for anti-slavery hatred before and during the U.S. Civil War. It remained a focus for anti-black racial hatred after the war. The small church building, which was meticulously disassembled and then reassembled on the campus of Southern Wesleyan University in Central, South Carolina, still stands today with the front door riddled with bullet holes fired at the building from angry racists. The irony of this symbol of racial justice currently standing in South Carolina, the heart of the Confederacy, is not lost on anyone!

Adam Crooks was not alone in sacrificing for this deeply spiritual, anti-slavery cause.

66 In Montgomery County [North Carolina], the Hulen family experienced a greater loss. They saw three sons summarily executed by Confederate vigilantes in retaliation for the family's antislavery principles and refusal to support the Confederate war effort. One was a boy of twelve, who was hanged as his helpless parents looked on in horror. Their older sons were shot. The floor of Lovejoy Wesleyan Methodist Chapel was permanently stained with their blood when the bodies of the three martyrs were laid there prior to their burial in a triple grave just four months before Robert E. Lee's surrender at Appomattox. (TWC, 51)

While all of this was going on in North Carolina, a different group of Wesleyan Methodists in Seneca Falls, New York, was fighting for women's voting rights. The announcement of the meeting read, "A Convention to discuss the social, civil, and religious condition and rights of woman [*sic*], will be held in the Wesleyan Chapel, at Seneca Falls, N.Y., on Wednesday and Thursday, the 19th and 20th of July, current; commencing at 10 o'clock" (TWC, 53). Here was born the Women's Suffrage Movement that ultimately led to voting rights for all women in the United States. Historians, Robert Black and Keith Drury, capture all of these founding stories well.

66 Wesleyan principles were consistent. The reformers who stood for the rights of slaves in the name of Christ took a stand for the rights of women in 1848 and backed it up in their own connection. Despite some initial confusion in the launch year of 1843, women enjoyed full voting rights as members in Wesleyan Methodist churches, and Wesleyan Methodist schools were all coeducational. In the years ahead, the denomination would make even more history by ordaining women to the Christian ministry. (TWC, 54-55)

These accounts of the beginnings of what is our denominational tribe bring great pride and humility to our hearts. (In fact, the Hulen family is part of Mike Hilson's family tree.) Today, many rightly hold in great reverence the blood and labor of those who sacrificed for the freedom and dignity of those historically and consistently oppressed. Many claim these roots, with good reason and intention, as grounds for steering the Church and Christians into today's versions of social activism. The argument is sound. We were born in activism, and therefore we must remain true to our roots and continue in activism.

> But the activism of our day is not the same as the activism of their day.

The activism taken on by Rev. Adam Crooks and the Hulen family was all about tearing down walls of separation based on nothing more than skin color, country, or region of origin, and gender. These people worked, bled, and died to defend the absolute Truth: "So in Christ Jesus you are all children of God through faith, for all of you who were baptized into Christ have clothed yourselves with Christ. There is neither Jew nor Gentile, neither slave nor free, nor is there male and female, for you are all one in Christ Jesus" (Gal. 3:26-28).

They worked, bled, and sometimes died to break down dividing walls.

> Unfortunately, current activism is working to rebuild the very walls that our ancestors died to tear down.

Generally, today's activism is intent on placing every person into a category that can be easily defined and painted with one broad brush as to that group's identity, beliefs, sins, and values. They work at convincing us that all white people are inherently racist or oppressive. They say that all African Americans are inherently oppressed and held back. They urge that all members of the LGBTQ+ community think and act in the same way. Furthermore, they insist that once placed in any defined category, white, black, heterosexual, LGBTQ+, conservative, liberal, etc., you can be defined and confined within that definition indefinitely. Any thoughts, opinions, preferences, or passions, which do not equate to the normative definition that the proponents of these categories have set, are dismissed as the outcome of oppression or oppressive tendencies and preferences. The thought of humans being simply "children of God" is completely foreign to this line of thinking (Gal. 3:26). Honestly, the all-are-created-equal crowd of the Crooks and Huleys would be dismissed today as mere, simple-minded people blinded by their own privilege. This insistence on demanding the recognition of categories of humans, and then applying the evils of each category's past to every member of that category in the present, causes current activism to bear a frightening similarity to Aldous Huxley's, *Brave New World.*

A BRAVE NEW WORLD

In his timeless work of satire, *Brave New World,* Aldous Huxley almost prophetically laid out the direction that our culture seems to be headed. In the opening line of his book, he describes, "A squat grey building of only thirty-four stories."[4] Did you catch that? A 34-story building is described as "squat?" To give perspective, that building is more than 10 yards taller than a football field is long from goal post to goal post. He gives a witty and simple word picture of the overgrown and self-important world he was about to enter into with the reader.

In the 1930s, he recognized the innate desire for *more* that seems to plague humanity and feed our ego as we climb higher. He ominously envisioned humanity being extracted from humans as society prioritized technological advancement over genuine moral progress. In his dystopian view of a world that has lost its sense of individuality, even the miracle of birth is reduced to an act of the state.

"And in exceptional cases we can make one ovary yield us over fifteen thousand adult individuals" (BNW, 8). He openly saw dividing walls between people as he spoke of working with "European material" or "some of the tropical Centres" or "Singapore" (BNW, 8-9). In this, he recognized the potential rise of a system that produces undistracted workers, in which the dad is the seed, the mother is the egg, and the governmental system is the Father (BNW, 24). He foreshadowed a sense of supremacy that is inevitable when we "gain control" of human reactions and interactions. A sense of control over the very course of nature is described here as, "What man has joined, nature is powerless to put asunder" (BNW, 22). He actually foreshadowed the almost inconceivable complexity of "defining" gender that we are now experiencing when he wrote, "a T for the males, a circle for the females and for those who were destined to become freemartins a question mark" (BNW, 13). All of this is put in place to meet the need of the government to produce more humans faster in their assembly lines due to the demand of the all-knowing "World State's motto, Community, Identity, Stability" (BNW, 1).

I get it! Our society is not that bad right now, but honestly, we are not that far off.

Huxley's book, *Brave New World*, begins by taking a group of students on a tour through the facility where they manufacture humans, or their "State Conditioning Centres" (BNW, 15). He speaks of genetically manufactured people with predispositions to things, like a warm climate, balance, or resistance to certain chemicals. There is disturbing imagery of how babies and children are taught to think and act according to their class. Particularly, how they are taught to think of other people.

> **66** Alpha children wear grey. They work much harder than we do, because they're so frightfully clever. I'm really awfully glad I'm a Beta, because I don't work so hard. And then we are much better than the Gammas and Deltas. Gammas are stupid. They all wear green, and Delta children wear khaki. Oh no, I *don't* [emphasis in original] want to play with Delta children. And Epsilons are still worse. They're too stupid to be able . . . . (BNW, 27-28)

Are you creeped out yet? Huxley called it. As technology has unimaginably increased the speed of shipping, the flow of information, and has even opened the possibility of inhabiting another planet, we seem to be simultaneously regressing into a caste system that teaches us how to think about others. This terrifying scenario is not limited to an old fictional tale. This, in fact, is the end goal of Marxism that has pervaded our educated class. Simply put, the philosophers of our day have discovered that if you create chaos within a culture, the culture will want the chaos to cease. And in the desperate growling hunger for comfort and stability, the population will wave the

white flag from the fetal position and ask someone—
anyone—to do the thinking for them. At this point of
desperation, society is prepared to accept any form
of structure that will bring even the illusion of peace.
Unfortunately, that structure has served to fabricate
false divisions that are destructive and foster hatred
and mistrust.

JESUS DYING FOR ALL, FOCUSED ON ONE

In the Gospel of Luke, we get helpful insight into how
Jesus viewed people.

> 66 One of the criminals who hung there hurled insults
> at him: "Aren't you the Messiah? Save yourself and
> us!" But the other criminal rebuked him. "Don't you
> fear God," he said, "since you are under the same
> sentence? We are punished justly, for we are getting
> what our deeds deserve. But this man has done
> nothing wrong." Then he said, "Jesus, remember me
> when you come into your kingdom. " Jesus answered
> him, "Truly I tell you, today you will be with me in
> paradise." (Luke 23:39-43)

Understand the moment. Jesus is hanging on the cross as a
result of a lying and manipulative group of ultra-legalistic,
religious oppressors. He has done nothing that would
deserve any punishment at all, especially not execution,
and is dying in front of everyone. He is bleeding, mocked,

thirsty, hungry, exhausted, and suffering. And why? He is dying for the forgiveness of all mankind.

> Jesus is literally dying for every person, in every place, at every time, in every circumstance.

But in that moment, dying for the masses, He somehow is focused on an individual. This is what we must achieve as Christians and as a Christian Church. There must be a balance between the chaotic preferences of the individualist, evangelist, and collectivist preferences of the institutionalized Church. A clear understanding of the necessity of an orderly institution balanced with the chaotic noise of conversions occurring at the most inopportune of moments is absolutely required.

THE INSTITUTION THAT SERVES THE MASSES

We must be able to see the usefulness in the moments of an institution that can serve and organize the masses of people who need and will find the grace of Jesus. Once they choose to follow Him, they will need direction, guidance, theology, doctrine, and structure. All of this will come from the institutionalized Church locally, nationally, and globally. These institutionalized practices will guarantee that our new follower of Christ, like our thief on the cross who has now become a child of God, will understand what we believe and why. These practices will teach disciplines and patterns that will grow the new believer in areas such as personal devotion, integrity, leadership, and the ability to communicate the Good News to others. Our institutionalized and collective understanding of God's Word, coupled with the individualized guidance of the Holy Spirit, will work together to move this thief to a fully sanctified believer and follower of the God of heaven.

THE EVANGELIST THAT SEES THE INDIVIDUAL

At the same time, we must battle against the collectivist tendency of institutionalized movements to require certain decorum, rites, and rituals performed in the right order and at the right places for organic conversion to happen. The collective denomination must make room for the movement-minded, chaotic force of nature that is the evangelist to remain focused on the individual who needs Jesus for the life change to take place. Surely, God would not desire to reach the lost in the middle of a bloody execution on a cursed hill. And yet, that is the precise location of what could be argued as the first conversion to Christianity. Even the 3,000 who were next to follow took place in the chaotic environment of a religious festival where those preaching the Good News of Jesus were assumed to be drunk (Acts 2:13, 41). Think about it. None of the earliest conversions to Christianity were achieved in organized institutions. They were all brought to faith in chaotic, secular, public, and often dirty places. These chaotic conversions resulted in a movement that still rocks the planet today! Furthermore, out of this individualistic chaos was birthed the institution of the Church.

One required the other, and that has not changed.

4

GOD IS DEAD . . . OR NOT?

66

The madman jumped into their midst and pierced them with his eyes. "Whither is God?" he cried; "I will tell you. *We have killed him—* you and I. All of us are his murderers. . . . Do we not feel the breath of empty space? Has it not become colder? . . . Do we smell nothing as yet of the divine decomposition? Gods, too, decompose. God is dead. God remains dead. And we have killed him."[1]

—Friedrich Nietzsche, *The Gay Science*

To the Jews who had believed him, Jesus said, "If you hold to my teaching, you are really my disciples. Then you will know the truth, and the truth will set you free."

—John 8:31-32

Theism | "Belief in the existence of one God viewed as the creative source of man and the world who transcends yet is immanent in the world."[2]

Atheism | "A disbelief in the existence of deity."[3]

Friedrich Nietzsche, the 19th-century German philosopher, arrogantly declared the death and end of God. His contemporary, Karl Marx, also a 19th-century German philosopher, said that "communism abolishes eternal truths, it abolishes all religion, and all morality."[4] Like Nietzsche, Marx called for the death of God and an end to religion as a whole. The thinking was simple. Religion is the problem, and rational reason is the solution. However, even Nietzsche seemed to understand that his "solution" of killing God would come at a great cost. In his quote at the beginning of the chapter, did you catch the emptiness? He said, "empty space," and "colder."[5] He was not clueless; he was fully sober about the ramifications of the death of God in culture. Nietzsche was, in fact, able to see the destructive force that was being unleashed when Marx did not.

The problem with the death of God theory is that it results in a fractured foundation with nothing of truth on which to stand. If there is no Creator God above all human philosophy, then there are no boundaries to contain the flaws of human philosophy. With no God, we lose the horizon upon which we can establish our balance. We are left to invent new rules that attempt to determine which way is up and which way is down. In the process of inventing new rules, based not on an unchanging God but on the shifting whims of individual thinkers or collective mobs, there will be an inevitable loss of horizon and the nauseating dizziness of no up or down, left or right.

This false belief in a utopia that lies hidden just beneath the abstract and unexplored concept of a world without religion—a world without God—has become a mystery box that society cannot help but try and open. Attempting to find a perfect world by ridding it of religion will never rid the world of God. By pretending He's not there, we worsen the problems we wish to be solved. We inevitably introduce increased confusion into an already broken and convoluted world.

> Let us keep in mind that Nietzsche's entire death of God theory was built at a desk, while the foundation for the Christian faith was built on a cross.

Enlightenment for Nietzsche began with his *accidental* discovery of Arthur Schopenhauer's *The World as Will and Representation* when he was 21-years old.[6] Deciding to kill

God from behind his desk with no tangible follow-up plan was a bit like getting rid of the doctor and letting the family dog diagnose your illness!

Not all enemies of faith are as direct and straightforward as Nietzsche. Eric Metaxas described the approach to religion in England during the time of William Wilberforce, who spent his life working to end slavery in Great Britain. British officials worked to accomplish this by advocating the powerful to "staunchly retain the outward trappings and forms of religion—which were all well and good and would help keep the lower classes better behaved—but it would deny religion any real power. Religion would be defanged and declawed quietly, not killed in front of the mobs"[7] This is a frighteningly accurate description of the American culture's relationship to the Church today. The current *truth* within Western culture is largely in agreement with Nietzsche and Marx.

> The god of reason and enlightenment has replaced the God of Scripture in the minds and philosophies of most modern thinkers and leaders.

The new religion of our day is a deeply held faith, and it is based entirely on faith, in godlessness and "defanged" religion. It is painfully obvious in today's debate that this irreligious religion acts in every way and shape like all other religions preceding it. It demands adherence to its own core theologies and punishes anyone who dares to defile its central deity, human reason.

To place a fine tip on the point, the following is a quote from an article published in *Time Magazine* in April of 1966:

> 66 Even within Christianity . . . a small band of radical theologians has seriously argued that the churches must accept the fact of God's death, and get along without him. . . . The current death-of-God group believes that God is indeed absolutely dead, but proposes to carry on and write a theology without *theos*, without god (emphasis in original).[8]

This group has done nothing but expand since this article was published nearly 60 years ago.

> Atheism is the new theism, and the human mind has become the new icon before which we are to bow, pray, and worship.

Therefore, in our current culture, the evangelist is to bring a reason-centered individual out of this theology lacking a God and into the acceptance of the actual living God who can give order and meaning to the thinker's thoughts. As current evangelists, we must learn to wield the weapon of iconoclasm, which is the rejection of the cherished beliefs of the god-is-dead or god-is-divisive theology that so pervades our culture. This practice is not new. In 1961, C. S. Lewis brilliantly described it this way:

❝ My idea of God is not a divine idea. It has to be shattered time after time. He shatters it Himself. He is the great iconoclast. Could we not almost say that this shattering is one of the marks of His presence? The Incarnation is the supreme example; it leaves all previous ideas of the Messiah in ruins. And most are "offended" by the iconoclasm; and blessed are those who are not.[9]

To be entirely clear on this, we must realize that Jesus was the ultimate iconoclast. The death of Jesus was an act of breaking down the false ideas of God held for centuries. Even now, every so often, it seems the Holy Spirit has to step in to do it again. As the institution of the Church hardens against the seemingly chaotic movement of the Holy Spirit through the evangelists among us, the iconoclasts must step forward and break the hardened exoskeleton to allow for the continued growth of the soft and pliable body of Christ.

So even as believers in Theos (God), we must at times check and re-center our theology. This practice is imperative as time slowly hardens the hot, free-flowing lava of a movement into the set and immovable stone of an institution. The stone may cool and harden in strange and broken ways. These can only be broken and thus repaired by the heat of a new eruption (movement) or the shaking of a great earthquake (revolution). Eruptive and earth-shattering moments like these do not have to be feared. Instead, the leaders of the institution can anticipate them if they understand the need for the movement. When both voluntarily submit, the result is a structure (institution) built with such disasters (movement) in mind. There is strength and protection (institution) from invading and destructive forces, and there is flexibility to move and sway when the ground beneath unexpectedly shakes (movement).

5

CLASSISM VERSUS GRACE

Aren't we all actually radical evangelists?

So in Christ Jesus you are all children of God through faith, for all of you who were baptized into Christ have clothed yourselves with Christ. There is neither Jew nor Gentile, neither slave nor free, nor is there male and female, for you are all one in Christ Jesus.

—Galatians 3:26-28

Classism | "Prejudice or discrimination based on class."[1]

Grace | "Unmerited divine assistance given man for his regeneration or sanctification."[2]

I (Mike) guess I was about 24-years old. I was sitting in a hotel room in Cincinnati, Ohio, where I attended a gathering of district youth ministry directors for our Christian tribe known as The Wesleyan Church. As I stared out the window from a pretty high floor, the double-decker bridge crossing the Ohio River mesmerized me. Being a country boy, I had never seen anything like that before. As I sat and prayed, the Holy Spirit began to break my heart. The question that kept repeating in my mind was, "How many of them know Him?" Thousands of people were crossing that bridge, and in the culture I currently lived in, no more than 20% knew of the love of Christ I had found and was called to proclaim.

I sat there fighting off tears as I yearned for the chance to tell them all about Jesus! Every fiber of my being wanted to go stand in the middle of that bridge and shout the name of Christ so they would all know. That pivotal moment, along with so many others, convinced me that I must find ways to make Christ known to everyone. Like so many before me, I had found the answer, or perhaps *the answer* found me, and they all needed to know Him!

The world was so simple at that moment. People need Jesus. I can honestly say that no clarifying words or categorizing structures entered my mind or my heart at that moment. There were no thoughts of white people or brown people, rich people or poor people, employed people or unemployed people, powerful people or unknown people. People—all people—need Jesus, and I had to find a way to introduce them to Him.

Those were simpler times.

Today, we are not allowed to think in such simplistic terms. If I were to go back to that hotel room today and watch the cars pass over that bridge, society tells me I would need to check my passion against my category.

Have I actually found the answer, or is my racial background just attempting to force everyone else into my idea of right and wrong?

Am I actually promoting freedom from sin, or am I simply imposing my version of freedom on others?

How dare I suggest that my religious preferences should be

heard or received by anyone else?

Perhaps, instead of evangelistic fervor, I am simply suffering from generational racism that has so deeply embedded itself into my psyche that I don't even know it's there.

These are the nagging questions that are taunting the passionate, religious leaders of our day. These questions arise from a ubiquitous philosophy that forces everyone into a category that is considered inescapably fixed and unarguably real. To these thinkers, debate is only a sign of privilege, and the desire to see people's lives made *better* is only a sign of internalized racism and/or classism.

> If the majority of those who know freedom in Christ are overly concerned with offending those who do not yet know freedom in Christ, then it is no wonder that fewer and fewer people each year are finding peace and hope in Jesus!

CLASSISM REBORN

The theories that are driving our social discourse these days are determined to rebuild the walls that global society and even global Christianity have spent the last two centuries attempting to tear down. The only difference is that today they would build the walls to hold people in rather than to keep people out. In their book, *Critical*

Race Theory, Richard Delgado and Jean Stefancic point out the following: "A third theme of critical race theory, the 'social construction' thesis, holds that race and races are products of social thought and relations. Not objective, inherent, or fixed, they correspond to no biological or genetic reality; rather, races are categories that society invents, manipulates, or retires when convenient."[3] This statement that seemed to foster the hope that we could one day achieve a unified and fair society is dashed a few pages later when delivering a "Critique of Liberalism" by stating that, "Many liberals believe in color blindness and neutral principles of constitutional law. They believe in equality, especially equal treatment for all persons, regardless of their different histories or current situations" (CRT, 26). On the surface, this hardly seems like a rebuke. However, on the next page, we read the following: "Only aggressive, color-conscious efforts to change the way things are will do much to ameliorate misery" (CRT, 27). This idea of race that they argue is not grounded in reality must be nonetheless used in "aggressive" ways to "change the way things are."

So, we must use a false division to erase real divisiveness?

Or, worse yet, we must increasingly highlight the false divisions and demand that everyone categorize humans into these false divisions in order to eradicate these false divisions?

If this leaves you a little perplexed, you are not alone.

In the book, *Cynical Theories*, Helen Pluckrose and James Lindsay point out the difference between the *theories* that seem to dominate our social conversation and traditional liberalism. "Liberalism values the individual and universal human values; Theory rejects both in favor of group identity and identity politics. Although left-leaning liberals tend to favor the underdog, liberalism across the board centers human dignity; Theory focuses on victim hood."[4] Reading this will shock many conservatives as they find themselves rising up in defense of the liberals. How is it that the liberal now sounds so conservative? The answer is simple. Like the Wesleyan abolitionists and Women's Right to Vote advocates, the liberals worked and bled to break down the categorization of human beings created by false narratives for the benefit of a few elites. For centuries, these groups have toiled under the belief that all humans are created equal by God to bring equality and freedom to humans who were for whatever reason treated as less than human.

But the activism of our day is different.

Now it seems we are being asked to reconstruct those dividing categories, even in the face of admission that they are not real, in order to . . . what? Punish? Demoralize? Divide? What is the predictable end of this process? We haven't even touched on intersectional theory that would insist that each person from any category become familiar with all possible combinations of categories within the human family and understand and appreciate the challenges of those lived experiences in such a way as to offend no one. The complexity and ambiguity we are being called to live within and function inside of is literally mind-numbing.

And we wonder why people are hesitant to share their faith?

It is actually stunning that anyone is willing.

For culture, society, and the Church, this isn't working!

LET'S TRY GRACE

Philip, like Andrew and Peter, was from the town of Bethsaida. Philip found Nathanael and told him, "We have found the one Moses wrote about in the Law, and about whom the prophets also wrote—Jesus of Nazareth, the son of Joseph." "Nazareth! Can anything good come from there?" Nathanael asked. "Come and see," said Philip. When Jesus saw Nathanael approaching, he said of him, "Here truly is an Israelite in whom there is no deceit."

—John 1:44-47

In this account, it is clear that Nathanael has a negative attitude toward people who come from the town and region of Nazareth.

Nathanael is a bigot.

When confronted, Philip does not scold Nathanael for his sin of bigotry. He just said, "Come and see." In other words, "Nathanael, once you meet Jesus, you will understand how much good can come from a place you consider beneath you." Then, when Jesus meets Nathanael, He does not confront him about his bigotry, classism, racism, or whatever-ism that has caused him to speak in such a demeaning way about a whole region of people. Jesus recognizes him as a man who is deceived about the value of people from Nazareth; nonetheless, he is honest and without "deceit." Jesus receives Nathanael in his broken, offensive, bigoted state, and then shows him the error of his ways by being *Truth* in front of him.

This is grace lived out.

This story of shifting perceptions and grace plays out over and over again in the life of Jesus and the story of the Acts Church in the following accounts:

- Jesus calls Matthew, a hated tax collector, to be a disciple. (Matt. 9:9-13)

- Jesus dines in the house of Zacchaeus, a known liar and cheat. (Luke 19:1-10)

- Jesus sits and talks with the Samaritan woman at the well. (John 4:1-42)

- Jesus tells the story of the Good Samaritan. (Luke 10:25-37)

- Jesus protects the woman caught in adultery. (John 8:1-11)

- Jesus sends His disciples to the "ends of the earth." (Matt. 28:18-20, Acts 1:8)

- The Holy Spirit falls on people from "every nation under heaven." (Acts 2:5)

- Philip is sent to share the Good News with an Ethiopian official. (Acts 8:26-39)

- The Holy Spirit calls Saul, a persecutor of the church, as his final apostle. (Acts 9:1-19)

- The Holy Spirit sends Peter to the home of a Roman centurion to share the Good News, and they receive the Holy Spirit. (Acts 10)

- The church in Antioch sends Paul and Barnabas out to share the Good News. (Acts 13:1-3)

- The Church accepts non-Jewish believers without "burden" to them. (Acts 15:1-35)

The list could go on and on.

Throughout the letters of Paul, Peter, John, James, and others whose names we do not know, this theme of all humanity finding grace through Jesus is repeated. Now, let's say something brutally honest. The Jewish people of Jesus' day were absolutely racist. But then again, so was every other definable people group of that day. The Jews believed firmly that they were God's chosen people. They had their Scriptures and history to tell them how the God of Abraham, Isaac, and Jacob had chosen, blessed, and protected them throughout their history. Therefore, they saw everyone else as lacking the honor of such a classification. The Romans, who had overtaken Jerusalem and were oppressing the Jews, also believed they were superior to all other groups of people on the earth. The Babylonians, Persians, Medes, Canaanites, Philistines, Egyptians, and every other people group that had attacked, enslaved, or oppressed Israel throughout the Old Testament, believed they were a superior people group.

But Jesus changed all of that.

Jesus did not argue that He had come to save *only* the Jewish people. He came to save *all people*. Jesus came to fulfill the promise given to Abraham that "all peoples on earth will be blessed through you" (Gen. 12:3). That ancient, all-but-forgotten promise was fulfilled when Jesus came through the Jewish people for all humans. Categories would be overridden by grace. Races would be overridden by grace. Past actions would be overridden by grace. Social distinctions would be overridden by grace.

Only grace has a graceful ending.

Now we realize that through the past 2,000 years,

Christians have been responsible for division, persecution, death, and even wars. But the overarching story of the Church has been one of grace. Yes, one can tell the story of the self-righteous popes who ordered the Crusades or the overzealous piety of kings who ordered the inquisition. One can point out the Christians who defended such vile evil as slavery and racism. One can hate those Christians who have chosen to side with a political party or a governmental system. But if we are honest, we cannot miss the fact that the vast majority of the story of the Church is one of grace. And when the story diverts into something else, it does so because its leaders have forsaken the God who called them.

This is why all the talk about philosophies and systems.

Every human philosophy and every human system of government will eventually fail.

But God—grace—never will.

Grace brings peace—in that order.

Grace is actually required for peace.

> **Peace cannot be found at the end of a spear or the exclamation point of a shouted slogan.**

Peace only can be found on the other side of a freely given grace. It is ironic that the most common chanted phrase in demonstrations seems to be, "No Justice, No Peace!" This phrase is not a hopeful one; it is actually a threat. "Give us what we want or we will burn it down!" The proper, hopeful slogan is actually, "No Grace, No Peace!" While we must protest and strive for societal change, and while we should not give peace to tyrants, oppressors, or dictators, we must realize that actual peace requires real grace.

Grace is only found when we, the evangelists, declare it.

To the oppressed, grace brings freedom from oppression.

To the oppressor, grace brings conviction of sin and insight into suffering.

To the suffering, grace brings the hope of healing in this world or the next.

To the powerful, grace brings hope of divine direction.

To the working, grace brings dignity in work.

To the broken, grace brings hope for a new start.

To the hopeless, grace brings the hope of a God who loves us all!

How, then, can they call on the one they have not believed in? And how can they believe in the one of whom they have not heard? And how can they hear without someone preaching to them? And how can anyone preach unless they are sent? As it is written: "How beautiful are the feet of those who bring good news!"

—Romans 10:14-15

We must be purveyors of grace in a world that is constantly selling brokenness, anger, violence, and hatred.

The act of being purveyors of grace is called evangelism.

The only question left is—How?

PART

WHAT CAN WE DO NOW?

> **66** When you know what that one thing is and desire nothing else, something dynamic is unleashed in the world. It can change a church, a community, even a nation.[1]
>
> —Mark Gorveatte, *Lead Like Wesley*

6

EVANGELISM ISN'T ACCIDENTAL

"

God's plan is to make much of the man, far more of him than of anything else. Men are God's method. The Church is looking for better methods; God is looking for better men.[1]

—**E.M. Bounds,** *Power Through Prayer*

As the Father has loved me, so have I loved you. Now remain in my love. If you keep my commands, you will remain in my love, just as I have kept my Father's commands and remain in his love. I have told you this so that my joy may be in you and that your joy may be complete. My command is this: Love each other as I have loved you. Greater love has no one than this: to lay down one's life for one's friends.

—John 15:9-13

Relationship | "The relation connecting or binding participants in a relationship."[2]

William Wilberforce (1759-1833) was a British politician and evangelist who is best remembered for his work to help end slavery in England and her colonies. While his political career began in 1780, everything changed for him in 1785 in what he deemed as his "Great Change."[3] It was then that he surrendered his life fully to Jesus Christ and followed the Methodist movement that John and Charles Wesley had set into motion. While Wilberforce had an incredible life of political achievement, he was not focused primarily on climbing the political ladder. Instead, he believed that his faith in a God who created all people called him to work at bringing freedom to those who could not fight for themselves. He believed that Christianity was the key to making society work in harmony on a spiritual level, and he also understood that it practically made sense on a human level.

Wilberforce had the desire to see two mammoth

goals come to fruition in his lifetime. He wanted to turn the world back to God, and to see the atrocity of the slave trade abolished in England and eventually around the world. In the course of this fight to rid England of slavery, he lost battle after battle; yet, he still pressed forward. We need to remember that abolishing slavery would have taken generational wealth out of the pockets of those whose votes were essential in parliament. This task that he believed God had called him to was far more than what seemed possible. But pent-up in that 5'2" frame was a savage, little honey badger that would not quit fighting until either he accomplished the mission or had no breath left in his lungs.

According to *Amazing Grace* by Eric Metaxas, here is a short list of what Wilberforce accomplished in his lifetime:

- He was the first man to have the audacity to raise the issue of the abolishment of the slave trade in the House of Commons.

- He had a Proclamation Society, which had as its main goal the "Reformation of Manners," which pointed society back to some of the main teachings of Jesus.

- He fought for better education for children.

- He fought to end unjust child labor practices.

- He worked to set forth prison reforms.

- He fought for better conditions for the poor.

Wilberforce worked his entire life, yet it was just days before his death that he saw slavery outlawed in Britain and its colonies in 1833. As a result of this single accomplishment, Wilberforce, through the power of the Holy Spirit, had literally changed history. Considering all his achievements, we will never actually know how many lives this man saved.

We love stories like this one. They inspire us, lift us up, and give us hope. Lives like the one that Wilberforce lived make us think that perhaps we could be a part of a movement like that one day. However, as we look at lives like his, it is easy to see the big strides and great accomplishments. But what lies beneath the greatness? What did a man who did so much for society do when the spotlight was not on him? What habits made William Wilberforce? What shaped such an unshakable character?

Although he seemed to battle sickness his entire life, he was extremely disciplined in his devotion to God. He believed that faith in Jesus was more important than life itself. With everything else that Wilberforce accomplished in his life, he chose first and foremost to be an uncompromising evangelist. He discovered a way to accomplish this evangelistic goal, even outside his legendary oratorical skills. Personally connecting people to Jesus was his most important responsibility.

> Rightly understood, this personal responsibility to evangelism is, in fact, the call of every follower of Jesus.

It seems that Wilberforce knew that he could not control whether society changed as a whole, but he could control his intentionality with individuals with whom he came into contact. He believed this evangelistic intentionality, coupled with God's will, would be enough to reach the people around him with God's love. No matter who you were to him, his goal was always to shift "the conversation around to the question of eternity" (AG, 167). This devotion to his faith took a higher priority than his career. Wilberforce loved Scripture and would recite Psalm 119 (yeah, the long one) on his walks home from Parliament (AG, 218). He was personally responsible for bringing people of influence like the Duke of Gloucester into a devoted relationship with Jesus (AG, 216).

His relationships with individuals were ultimately the springboard for his achievement. In his book, *Amazing Grace*, Eric Metaxas writes about Wilberforce's meticulous lists of people that he kept and added to frequently (AG, 167). These lists consisted of people who knew Jesus and would need encouragement, as well as people who didn't know Jesus yet and would need an introduction.

> **❝** And so, everywhere he went, and with everyone he met, he tried, as best he could, to bring the conversation around to the question of eternity. Wilberforce would prepare lists of his friends' names and next to the entries make notes on how he might best encourage them in their faith, if they had faith, and toward a faith if they still had none. He would list subjects he could bring up with each friend that might launch them into a conversation about spiritual issues. He even called these subjects and questions "launchers" and was always looking for opportunities to introduce them. (AG, 167)

With all of Wilberforce's influence and achievements, you would think he had more important things to do than track his relationships in an effort to lead more people to Jesus. Of course, he did not seem to think so. Wilberforce was witty and charming. When he was with people, he was not lazy in language or absent in the interactions. He was present and focused on the one in front of him. He wished to speak the language of the ones he was trying to reach. He wanted to understand them before shoving Scripture in their faces or telling them how they should change their lives. He seemed to believe what Ralph Waldo Emerson would say a few hundred years later: "Every man I meet is my superior in some way, and in that I learn from him."[4]

As followers of Jesus and believers in His forgiving grace, we often want to see some sort of grand-scale, evangelistic movement. We want to see the Billy Graham event with one million people in attendance like there was in South Korea. We want viral videos about the gospel, and we want churches filled to the brim. We pray for the lost world, and we cast out the biggest net we can afford, hoping that it does not land in lonely, empty water. We spend thousands of dollars on mailers. We use Facebook and YouTube ads, and we tweet and promote. We attend conferences that tell us how to organize and attract more people. Then we come home and sit in offices and boardrooms making plans for our plans, only to end up bewildered when people are not coming to know Jesus through all our efforts. We want to see a movement, but we overlook individuals in favor of the crowds. We miss the simple truth that it is the people who make up the crowds. As I heard in a seminar once, "It takes each of us to make all of us."

The problem is when we try to draw in the masses before we come to know the individuals. William Wilberforce's legendary oratory in front of crowds was fueled and empowered by actions when he was face to face with them individually. The Holy Spirit moves in the application of Jesus' commands to love God and love people, not in the aspiration of setting forth a grand-scale movement. We believe the integrity and sincerity of Wilberforce on the matter of reaching the lost, one person at a time, was the power behind his achievements.

CHOOSING RELATIONSHIPS OVER METHODS

The problem with choosing methods of evangelism over personal relationships is that what you win someone *with* is what you will win someone *to*. Therefore, if someone is brought to Jesus predominantly through a method that is missing real, relational depth, how can we expect them to introduce someone else to a faith that is dependent on a deep relationship with God and people? If won by those who love crowds and not individuals, how can we expect them to communicate a faith rooted in a God who loves the individual? Smart and creative methods that lack true, relational depth may work on some levels. However, once these movements grow too large, they begin to break down into nothing more than shallow events that soon die, along with the shallow method from which they were produced.

The *training* on how to follow Jesus begins the moment a person enters into a relationship with a Christ-follower. People care less about what you say or what you proclaim and more about who you are and what you do. Like a child attempting to figure out the world, new Christians or those *on the fence* are watching what you do with an intensity they do not even realize yet. By watching a Christ-follower, they learn how to speak about their story and Scripture. They learn how much to listen and how much to speak. They learn which "vine" to connect with (John 15). Beginning a Kingdom movement starts in the heart and actions of the individual. That initial heart and those first actions determine where the movement will go and how long it will last. Time will promote or expose us all because, eventually, what we become is precisely what we replicate.

> The example of our lives should over-deliver on the promises that come out of our mouths.

Francis Chan so clearly illustrated this when he said the following: "A movement starts when the founder really knows Jesus. You know how movements die? When the followers only know the founder."[5]

Jesus understood that more is caught than taught. He opened up His entire life and allowed His disciples to put Him under a microscope. The way Jesus lived was the way He wanted them to live. Jesus was intentional about His relationships with His disciples. Likewise, William Wilberforce was intentional with those he wished to reach.

At this point, you might be saying, "This does not seem to answer the question of how to effectively evangelize." Oh, but it does! We would describe a true evangelistic movement this way:

A multiplied and compounded surrender to God—set in motion by the private and public actions of a few motivated individuals—that has spread from person to person until a movement ensues.

Strategically and practically speaking, investing heavily in *good soil*—or solid people—provides the most return for our efforts. It gives a strategy to reach people in which you never leave your *warm market*, those already in your sphere of influence. It is choosing to be more than an inch deep and a mile wide. It is choosing to be the person with deep and strategic relationships that compound in their depth and scope over time so it can be replicated and expanded to and by others. Rather than being the person that boastfully handed out 300 business cards at the last attended event (Don't be that guy!), choose to be the person who got to really know one or two new people. We all love the person who shows us real interest. So, if we would stop trying so hard to be *interesting* and instead work at being *interested*, maybe people would get curious about who we are and why we are so different from everyone else.

Spiritually speaking, God's math is different. It is as if He is saying, "If you take care of the ministry, I will take care of the opportunity." If you focus on the one in front of you, you will grow, become better, and set the example for the ones who come after you. You take care of the person in front of you, and I will take care of the masses of people around you. You take care of your devotion, and I will take care of the miracles. You plant the seed, and I will make the tree. In Old Testament terms, you search for Gomer, because I told you to go get her, and I'll take care of the Jewish people and their heritage (Hos. 1-3).

> ## Never overlook the one in pursuit of the many.

It is all a matter of trusting God by playing the part we were designed to play while fully believing He will take care of the variables and outcomes we cannot control. The problem is that we are too accustomed to the microwave. The oven is less appealing, and the slow smoker is out of the question! We struggle to find the line where God's part stops and ours begin, so we take back control. Then the movement that began with life and strength dies tough and hard, ruined by our attempt to *cook* it too fast. Yes, we need to participate in our own rescue. We must never just twiddle our thumbs and wait for God to fix it all. We must remember that we cannot get this done with our own *brilliance*. We need His empowerment.

PRACTICAL PROCESS

We must intentionally choose not to lose touch with the people we meet. We have to be careful not to barrel past the opportunities to reach people that God places in front of us every single day while praying that He would allow us to reach someone. We cannot just passively greet the sales clerk and hope they do not feel like talking or walk right by the homeless person with a past that would shatter our hearts if we knew their story. We must never neglect our own family because our busyness is so important. If we are not intentional, we could even miss our kids because we cannot stop thinking of the crowds. Instead, it is the list with the reminders set on your phone to reach out. It is the calls on the birthdays and remembering the anniversaries. It is the unexpected sending of ideas, books, or gifts that they will appreciate. It is the calls or texts when they cross your mind. It is praying specifically for them and sharing what God said rather than flippantly saying, "I will pray for you." It is not complicated, but it requires effort. You may be thinking, "I cannot add another thing to my plate." OK, even if that is true, I know plenty of people who do far more than this to sell insurance or a product they sort of believe in; yet, we will not do it to save souls?

We do not need more brilliant people with brilliant theories; we have plenty of that. However, we lack leaders who fully understand the mission because they are not in the trenches themselves. We need people who can say, "Follow me as I follow Christ," not, "Follow me because, on paper, this plan looks bulletproof." Time always exposes the foundation built on sand, and it reveals the foundation built on the rock. The Holy Spirit moves when we apply His commands. His miracles live in the selfless pursuit of souls. As we rush past the one in front of us to get to the big plan we have laid out, we run past the person for which the plan was designed. Instead, we must intentionally choose to grow in our understanding of the world we wish to serve.

The good news is that as the world and Church become inundated with cheap marketing tactics and flooded email inboxes, a simple phone call has become a lot more valuable. Honestly, it's another's lack of consistency that makes it so easy to stand out from the crowd and be the person that people turn to when they start to contemplate the eternal. (Remember that everyone eventually considers eternity!) In sales, they say, "The fortune is in the follow-up." It is no different in leading people to Jesus. The results are in the patient and thoughtful persistence of the one who desires to influence the other. You might say, "Well, that is manipulation!" No. Manipulation is getting people to do what you want them to do. Influence is helping people find what they have been looking for all along.

What a person desires is unfailing love.

—Proverbs 19:22

ACTION POINTS

Consider the following readily available resources and insights:

- Read books like *How to Win Friends & Influence People* by Dale Carnegie, *Talking to Strangers* by Malcolm Gladwell, *Becoming a Person of Influence* by John Maxwell, *Never Split the Difference* by Chris Voss, *The Art of Connection* by Michael J. Gelb, etc. Remember, the book you do not read will not help you.

- Find out what the people you want to reach are doing, and learn about it so you can add value and ask great questions. This builds bridges and gives way to effortless conversation.

- Attend classes on influencing people like Chris Voss' master class or a course taught by Tony Robbins that teaches strategies on connecting with people. Stop being weird. Relationship building is a skill. Develop it.

- Make your list and write out your "launchers" (subjects and questions to launch you into conversation).

  TIP: Make a *Saved* list of those you want to pray for and encourage. Make an *Unsaved* list with launchers next to their name. Each day during your devotion time, choose one name from each list and pray for them. Reach out to them that day.

  RULE: No one leaves your list until they die.

> They simply transition from the unsaved category to the saved.

- Remember that you will face rejection and frustration. Be willing to look stupid or naive. Just like anything else, there is a learning curve. Embrace it.

7

EGO MUST BE ABANDONED

66

If you and I agree, I'm not accomplishing anything by trying to convince you of what you already know. The way you resolve that is, you invite somebody to the table who disagrees with you so you'll understand why they have that point of view. Then perhaps, you would figure out a solution to dissuade their fears.[1]

—Daryl Davis

Above all, love each other deeply, because love covers over a multitude of sins.

—1 Peter 4:8

Ego | "The self especially as contrasted with another self or the world."[2]

Daryl Davis is an incredibly talented African American musician as well as an author, activist, speaker, and actor who lives in the suburbs of Washington, D.C.[3] After an encounter with a Ku Klux Klan (KKK) member, he became obsessed with one simple question: "How can you hate me when you don't even know me?"[4] In order to discover the answer to this question and begin to break the hatred that was obviously present, Davis began building relationships with members and leaders of the KKK. These were people who should have been his enemies. These were people who chose to hate him simply because he was born with different skin color. By societal standards, he should have stayed far away, and he should have hated them back. But Daryl Davis couldn't let his curiosity rest. As a result, he began pursuing those who questioned his value as a human being. He chose to abandon his own ego and instead pursued conversation, relationship, and understanding. In the process, he took the posture of Jesus.

Let's pause for one second. That is ridiculous. Think about it. Today, we willingly choose to ostracize people for a slip of the tongue or an honest disagreement in beliefs. We hold grudges, and we love to say, "Never forget." Instead, this man literally entered into generations of unwarranted hate with an open mind and outstretched arms. If this doesn't look like Jesus, then what does?

In the documentary, *Accidental Courtesy: Daryl Davis, Race & America,* Davis tells the following story. In the 1990s, Davis was a guest speaker on the *Geraldo* show with "Neo-Nazis and some Klan." There were two daughters, Erica and Erin Puig, one 12 and the other in her teens, and they spoke of how they would join the Klan just like their mother and father. Some time after this, the father of those girls was sentenced to 10 years in federal prison. When Davis heard about it, he wanted to see how he could serve this family. He tracked down the phone number and called the mother, Tina Puig. As Davis recounts this moment, he described how she "cursed me up one side and down the other." She was furious that he even had the nerve to call her. He responded, "Tina, shut up and listen to me for a second." He proceeded to tell her that he could help them. As it turned out, he flew with Tina and her daughters to Chicago and then drove them to Marion, Illinois, to the federal penitentiary where their husband/father was imprisoned so that they could visit him. Davis said, "Nobody in the Klan had ever done that for them before." Some time later, while sharing a stage with Davis on Martin Luther King Jr. Day, Tina gave Davis a heartfelt hug and said to the crowd, "I do believe God does work through people, other human beings, and He most certainly uses Daryl Davis as an instrument, because that man has touched a lot of lives." Tina and her daughters left the Klan. Their view of God shifted once they saw someone act like the one they have heard about from the pulpits.[5]

Davis surrendered to his own ego, to his right to be offended, and to the God of heaven, which allowed him to bless even those who denied his value because of the color of his skin. This kind of reconciliation through surrender has become the life pursuit of Daryl Davis. He seeks out ways to establish relationships with people who have sworn to hate him. An example of this is when he let the Klan use his bus one time for a rally when they couldn't find one to rent. The secret power of this kind of surrender is sincerity. Davis doesn't do these things because of some self-righteous agenda. He seems to have no expectation of reciprocation of the grace he shows these men and women. But then again, that's the definition of grace. In Ryan Holiday's book, *Ego is the Enemy*, Goethe said, "What matters to an active man is to do the right thing; whether the right thing comes to pass should not bother him."[6]

The abandonment of our ego allows us to serve those who will never return the favor. It allows us to give in the way we've been given to by Jesus. Far too many of us are obsessed with ourselves. We are engulfed in a pattern of thinking that revolves around what we will receive in return for our investment. The problem with this is we think about people in the same way we think about a paycheck. If I put in *this*, I expect *that* in return. However, an insistence on reciprocation isn't grace. Furthermore, it falls significantly short of the unconditional love shown to us and commanded from us by our heavenly Father. Service with the expectation of payment is no more than love with a caveat. It's imitation grace with a comma and a *but*. From the cross of Calvary, Jesus said, "It is finished" (John 19:30). The sentence ends with a period, not a comma and a *but*. His command is that we lay down our lives for those He created. We don't need better mailers and more creative Facebook ads. We need more people willing to lay down their lives and let go of their egos so they can establish life-giving and grace-showing relationships with their enemies.

Daryl Davis has collected hundreds of Klan robes given to him by people who had once trusted in their own hatred. Through the unusual, ego-less surrender of this one man, they were able to find grace, healing, and trust. Hundreds of people have seen the love of Jesus through the almost ridiculous pursuit of a man who cared more about their stories than their affiliations. He cared more about the individual behind the robe than he did about demanding justice for the misguided lives who burned crosses and hated humans who looked different from them. Davis saw beyond the hate; he saw the human. He saw beyond the malice; he saw the meaning. He saw through the hateful facade; he saw the value. He saw beyond the robe; he saw the person. He pointed out the difference between their hatred and his love when he said to one Klansman that "there had to be two Jesus Christs. . . . There's yours and there's mine. You have to light the way for your Jesus Christ. My Jesus Christ lights the way for me."[7] What sets us apart is not that we have a louder voice or a more compelling argument. What sets us apart is the relinquishment of self. It's the unobstructed pursuit of the soul for the sake of loving and understanding. It's easy to preach on Sunday to those who will *amen* just about anything we say, but what about everyone else?

In our culture right now, it seems that everyone is fighting to be heard and fighting to win. This is not an effective strategy for anyone or any movement. We cannot gain understanding if we fight to win. As followers of Christ, we must fight to understand. Debate is fine as long as it has direction and purpose; however, debate for the sake of debate is no more than an hour of empty words. Do you want to set yourself apart and reach someone? Then fight to understand them. Fight for the chance to know them. Once we do that, we have a fighting chance of seeing them set free by the grace of our Savior.

> **It's time to stop fighting to win and stop demanding justice through vengeance.**

Instead, choose to surrender to the Jesus that listens to our hearts with compassion in His heart.

Want to reach them?

Serve them.

ACTION POINTS

Consider the following questions in your own life:

- When is the last time you willingly put yourself in an uncomfortable situation to serve someone?

- Have you ever laid aside your ego in order to reach out to someone (stranger, friend, family) knowing you would be insulted or pushed aside?

- When was the last time you stopped thinking of what you wanted to say and instead looked into the eyes of the person you wanted to help?

- Can you intentionally stop the chatter in your mind long enough to hear what the person across from you has to say?

- Are you willing to take the time to discern the real meaning behind someone else's words, especially if you disagree with them?

8

A WALK WORTH FOLLOWING

66

People do not choose to become spiritual leaders. Spiritual leadership flows out of a person's vibrant, intimate relationship with God. You cannot be a spiritual leader if you are not meeting God in profound, life-changing ways.[1]

—Henry & Richard Blackaby,
Spiritual Leadership

Do you not know that in a race all the runners run, but only one gets the prize? Run in such a way as to get the prize.

—1 Corinthians 9:24

Real | "Of or relating to fixed, permanent, or immovable things; not artificial, fraudulent, or illusory."[2]

His name is Anthony. My (Curtis) best friend in high school was a 6'9" black guy named Anthony Anderson. Now, just to make sure you have the right picture in your mind, I'm a 5'4" white guy. As we walked around together, we received plenty of literal *up* and *down* looks. After high school, I didn't go to college. Instead, I stayed home to drop out of community college and smoke weed while Anthony went off to play basketball for Morgan State University.

For some reason, though, Anthony would always reach out to me and ask how I was doing. He would call just to catch up. This was strange to me. Anthony had started this new, exciting, and busy life. Why would he be reaching out to me? I didn't have anything at all going on. I should have been the one reaching out to him. Nonetheless, he was consistent.

Anthony was nearly 7 feet tall and 260 pounds after

his first semester in college. He was a giant. It seemed like he had it all figured out, and he was on top of the world. To me, he was a larger-than-life model of what was possible for people. But I learned quickly that even superheroes could fall. I got a call one night around 9 p.m. that Anthony was in the hospital. They found cancer. It was leukemia. My mind raced with questions. Anthony can't have cancer; it's *Anthony*! Little did I know, his energy and appetite had been decreasing for weeks, and he had grown lumps on the back of his neck, some bigger than golf balls. He was going to start treatment soon, and I had to go see him.

That week, I shaved my head just before I left for the hospital, hoping to make him feel better about the side effects of chemotherapy. But what I didn't account for is that Anthony is tall, dark, handsome, and has a voice like James Earl Jones. Furthermore, bald works great for him. I, on the other hand, am small, pale, and fragile. I looked more like Baby New Year (Google it).

Over the coming months, Anthony began to wither away. But he fought, and then, miraculously, there was a turn for the best. He came to my house one day, and he lifted his shirt to show me where the tubes had been removed from his chest and stomach. He was cancer-free! That week, he registered for classes again at Morgan State and was ready to start his new life when the hospital called. He was driving his new red Mustang down the highway when he heard the nurse on the other end of the phone say, "Mr. Anderson, the cancer is back. We need you to come in immediately to start treatment." In disbelief and feeling absolutely gutted, he threw his phone out of the window and sped to my house. He told me the news and asked if he could use my phone. I listened as he called his mom and said, "Well, mama, let's get ready for round two." I'm watching him, sitting on the side of my bed, telling his mom that it was "all going to be OK." It felt as if the floor had just been taken out from under me. But there was something different that I noticed about him. I could see the pain in his face. I could feel the disbelief and heartache he was feeling, but as he said those words to his mother, I could hear the *peace* in his voice. This moment has never left me. He had something I didn't. I always knew Anthony was athletic. I always knew he had a strong mind. I always knew he was smart and driven. But on this particular night, I saw that Anthony possessed something I didn't even understand and something that perhaps not many people I met had.

As time went on, his battle got more intense. He would sometimes spend up to four months in the hospital, barely leaving the bed. On multiple occasions, I would call and start to complain about my day. I would stop myself, almost blushing because I was so embarrassed by my thoughtlessness, and then I would say, "How are *you* doing?" His response: "I'm doing good, man." Then he would proceed to tell me about the tough parts of his day, but he almost always found something positive. One of his little lines was: "God's got me." He would always tell me about this little girl who had cancer in the room down the hallway. He would go to her room every single day. "She's my friend," he would always say. He would go there just to brighten her day. I think she brightened his, too. He would always tell me, "I don't know if I'll make it to tomorrow, but I know I can make her day a little bit better today." I still remember the way he cried the day she lost her battle; I had never heard him like that before.

Anthony's response, "I'm doing good, man," was not a fake response. He would tell me when his days were terrible, but everything he did and said was laced with joy somehow. There was a peace he had when facing death, which I couldn't seem to find when I was stuck in traffic on the way home from work. He had been battling for four years. He had bone marrow transplants, chemo, and, on multiple occasions, the doctors told him there was no hope. He was a whopping 139 pounds. For perspective, I was *also* 139 pounds. Remember, he's a foot and a half taller than me! He was deathly ill, battling cancer, and I was pathetically broke trying to sell insurance. Some days, I didn't even have gas money to drive home, so I would drive to Anthony's house and stay there. We were a pitiful little pair. We would stay up late and dream about cars, money, and, one day, marrying tall Swedish women.

I remember starting a book for Anthony. The doctors

told him he didn't have much time left. I would go to his house after work, and he would talk, and I would type. We did this for months. We cried and laughed until we almost peed. Well, I almost peed. He literally peed. One night, in particular, I came to his house after a failed sales presentation. He was in his bed, frail, and hooked up to so many tubes that he looked like a science experiment. He had enough medication to fill a pharmacy on his nightstand. But on this night, he was listening to a gospel song. I still don't remember the song, but I remember his face. It was soaked with tears. The tears were pouring down his face, and his hands were in the air. I thought something was wrong until I realized that he was thanking and praising this God who I had not met . . . yet.

Anthony is a real Christian.

Anthony knew Jesus, and although he was not exactly surrendered to the will of God as a teenager, his faith was strong. His life opened the door to me experiencing Christ for the first time. I found God in the deepest part of Anthony's life. He had told me about God before, and I was uninterested, to say the least. But he showed me God in his pursuit of our friendship when he went away to college. He showed me God when he was lifting up his mom on the phone that night. He showed me God in the face of death, loss, and hopelessness. He showed me God in the way he walked down that hall to see that little girl when the nerves in his feet hurt so badly it would bring him to tears.

> His life made me question everything I
> believed. I wanted whatever it was that
> he had.

So one night, after Anthony had fallen asleep, I walked into the other room with a Bible I had recently purchased. I read Matthew 7:21-23:

❝ Not everyone who says to me, "Lord, Lord," will enter the kingdom of heaven, but only the one who does the will of my Father who is in heaven. Many will say to me on that day, "Lord, Lord, did we not prophesy in your name and in your name drive out demons and in your name perform many miracles?" Then I will tell them plainly, "I never knew you. Away from me, you evildoers!"

Those words sank in that night. Many people think they know Him, but they don't. I kept reading.

❝ Therefore everyone who hears these words of mine and puts them into practice is like a wise man who built his house on the rock. The rain came down, the streams rose, and the winds blew and beat against that house; yet it did not fall, because it had its foundation on the rock. But everyone who hears these words of mine and does not put them into practice is like a foolish man who built his house on sand. The rain came down, the streams rose, and the winds blew and beat against that house, and it fell with a great crash. (Matt. 7:24-27)

These verses terrified me and encouraged me all at the same time. My heart shattered into pieces, but my soul sprang out of hibernation. Somehow, at that moment, it finally clicked. While we were both trying to build our house, the difference between Anthony and me was that he chose the rock, and I chose the beach. He would always bring up that verse in Revelation (3:16) about being "lukewarm," and he would say that he just wanted a faith that was *real*. I finally understood what that meant. Oswald Chambers said, "If through a broken heart, God can bring His purposes to pass in the world, then thank Him for breaking your heart."[3]

Tears streamed down my face as I thought about the people I knew who might never meet God. God told me, "It's time to do something." It was as if my eyes were finally open to my responsibility, and I realized that people I loved might go to hell if I didn't do something about it. I was scared because of the reality of hell, and the purity, justice, and power of God. However, my soul was on fire because I could see how to be a part of the solution.

That joy he had in the trial, I finally got it.

That peace he had on the phone with his mom that night many years ago, I finally understood it.

The next nine months were the craziest nine months of my life. I devoured Scripture. I prayed, fasted, read, served, and acted as if the Bible was what we say it is—the living Word of God.

I saw answered prayers for salvation.

I saw answered prayers for family.

I saw the unexplainable.

I experienced the miraculous.

I expected God to move.

My faith was like a child who expected a response from their father.

I was all in.

On the day of my baptism, Anthony showed me God again. Out of the water and with my towel in hand, I walked to the back of the sanctuary. I broke down once again when I saw that frail giant hunched over in the back of the room. I asked him, "How did you get here?" He replied: "I drove. Man, I wasn't going to miss this." He was in no shape to drive. He could barely sit without falling over. But Anthony had something different, and I finally had it, too.

I don't tell this story so that we can idolize Anthony. (He's doing great now, by the way. He's cancer-free and thriving in his career. I always forget that part when telling his story. Would you believe we both ended up marrying tall, blonde, Swedish women? Our dreams came true!) I can easily write a chapter on his flaws, just as he could on mine. I tell his story to illustrate that I am sitting at my desk writing a book on evangelism, hoping to reach more people because of the pursuit of God shown to me by Anthony. His investment in me led me to Jesus and will hopefully be multiplied in my life. It is my prayer that my life can have the same effect on someone else. Remember, God's math is different. In His Kingdom, depth produces scope, and the more depth we have, the bigger the movement we can see. Our opportunity to see people come to Christ lies in walking alongside them and showing them the way. It's in the transparency and the depth of the relationship that lives are transformed. All too often, we rely on the sermon and the small group when God has called us to the relationship and the deeper life.

I revisit these moments with Anthony often, and I am led to repent. I am led to turn back to devotion and depth so that my life lines up with my mouth because I want to live a life worth following.

Don't you?

ACTION POINTS

Ask yourself some questions:

- If someone who did not know Christ followed you and replicated your actions, would it produce disciples or contradiction and confusion?

- What are the habits in your life you would be embarrassed to have revealed?

- How can you alter your life choices to be the example that could draw someone else to Christ?

- Is your walk with God worth following?

9

A MOVEMENT THAT ENDURES

66

If you shut up truth and bury it under the ground, it will but grow, and gather to itself such explosive power that the day it bursts through it will blow up everything in its way.[1]

—Emile Zola,
quoted in *Ego is the Enemy*

And so it was with me, brothers and sisters. When I came to you, I did not come with eloquence or human wisdom as I proclaimed to you the testimony about God. For I resolved to know nothing while I was with you except Jesus Christ and him crucified. I came to you in weakness with great fear and trembling. My message and my preaching were not with wise and persuasive words, but with a demonstration of the Spirit's power, so that your faith might not rest on human wisdom, but on God's power.

—1 Corinthians 2:1-5

Revival | "A period of renewed religious interest; restoration of force, validity, or effect."[2]

The religious landscape of England was changed during the 1700s by the evangelistic work of two brothers, John and Charles Wesley. From high-minded beginnings at Oxford to the depths of a shaken faith and vision following ministry failure in Savannah, Georgia, the Wesley brothers were not off to a good start. Once returned to England from their disastrous time in Georgia, they took up with a group of Moravians whose faith had impressed them during a storm at sea on the way to the American colonies. At one point, John Wesley traveled to Germany to personally meet with their leader, Count Zinzendorf. He was so impressed with the group that "when asked at the town gate of his intentions, he said he was 'going to see the place where the Christians lived.' At the time, he thought of the Moravians 'as the only true Christians in the world.'"[3] Upon return to London, he attended a prayer meeting.

66 In the evening I went very unwillingly to a society in Aldersgate-Street, where one was reading Luther's preface to the Epistle to the Romans. About a quarter before nine, while he was describing the change which God works in the heart through faith in Christ, I felt my heart strangely warmed. I felt I did trust in Christ, Christ alone for salvation: And an assurance was given me, that he had taken away *my* sins, even *mine*, and saved *me* from the law of sin and death (emphasis in original).[4]

That was the beginning of what would become the Methodist revivals that swept across England and, ultimately, across the world.

As the revival began, the societal leaders in England were concerned at the thought of a new religious movement launching with such fervor. England had been the site of numerous bloody conflicts between Catholics, Protestant Anglicans, and Calvinists. At this point, the last thing leaders of the nation wanted was another bloody, religious fight. But they soon found that this revivalist movement was different. "Methodists were not new Levellers: the importance of Methodism was that it was simultaneously subversive and conservative, a dynamic Revivalist movement but also a teacher of respectability, obedience and sobriety—in short, politeness."[5]

As the Wesley brothers were founding and shepherding

their new Methodist movement in the mid-1700s, they could not have imagined that the "respectability, obedience and sobriety" they were teaching would play such a vital role in protecting England after their deaths. In the later 1700s, revolutions broke out across the European and American landscapes. In the French Revolution (1789-1799), like those a century later in Russia and China, the first institution to be dismissed and dismantled was the Church. In contrast, England and the American colonies retained religious beliefs at very high levels. In France, society devolved into the "Reign of Terror,"[6] when group after group was slaughtered, some at the guillotine, for not being part of the latest *right* way of thinking. At the very time of the French Revolution, England was in the midst of muddling through the loss of the American colonies, a weakened monarchy, and a diminished global landscape. However, England did not fall into revolutionary chaos. In fact, when the unpopular King George III began to suffer "severe mental confusion . . . the public reaction seems to have been one of sympathy."[7] While these more stable and graceful reactions to societal faltering and royal weakness cannot be fully credited to the more *polite* outcomes of the Methodist revivals, the power of this movement in both England and the newly formed United States cannot be dismissed. One writer put it this way when he said, "As a result, eighteenth-century England witnessed a remarkable spiritual awakening that historians believed saved the British Isles from a bloody revolution similar to that which the French experienced at the hands of the deists, agnostics, and atheists."[8]

John Wesley did not start a megachurch in the center of London, nor did he put all his eggs in the basket of politics and try to change the system from the inside out. Instead, he chose to climb down out of his high Episcopal pulpit and on top of a tombstone (sometimes his own father's tombstone) to preach Jesus to working-class people headed home from an exhausting day's work. He reached them one at a time until there was a following. From there, he used his relationships, testimony, and desire to serve in the power of the Holy Spirit to connect and empower the people around him, which, in turn, reached the people around them. In his ministry, John Wesley took the words of Martin Luther to heart.

> **❝** Faith is God's work in us, that changes us and gives new birth from God. (John 1:13). It kills the Old Adam and makes us completely different people. It changes our hearts, our spirits, our thoughts and all our powers. It brings the Holy Spirit with it. Yes, it is a living, creative, active and powerful thing, this faith. Faith cannot help doing good works constantly. It doesn't stop to ask if good works ought to be done, but before anyone asks, it already has done them and continues to do them without ceasing.[9]

John Wesley preached a gospel of faith to anyone who

would listen. He connected them to one another and the Vine of Scripture (John 15), the power of the Holy Spirit, and a relationship with Jesus. Although his personal piety and the devotion required of his ministers were extreme by today's standards, he did not work to constrict his followers. Instead, he empowered Spirit-filled yet unqualified people to fight the societal ills in the communities in which they were most passionate. He allowed the messy, unpredictable, powerful move of God to shift culture and give England a glimpse of Jesus. As a result, his "was a practical religion that worked to reform those areas of society where there was most moral bankruptcy and suffering."[10]

It is now our time to step up and find our hearts "strangely warmed" by the power of God's Holy Spirit and the love of Jesus Christ. It seems that the Church has drifted so far into the arenas of philosophy, politics, social theory, and social justice that our central focus on the saving grace of Jesus and transforming power of the Holy Spirit has been severely diminished, if not lost altogether.

This trend must be reversed.

That reversal will only come and be sustained by following John Wesley's example as he followed Christ. If we want to see a movement—people saved and transformed—and we want that movement to last, Jesus gave us the only method to sustain such a life-altering, powerful reality.

In John 15, 16, and 17, Jesus is giving his send-off speech to his closest friends and followers. He is giving them warnings, encouragement, and marching orders. He is summing up his time with them over the last few years in just a few stories, analogies, and lessons. In John 15:5, Jesus said, "I am the vine; you are the branches. If you remain in me and I in you, you will bear much fruit; apart from me you can do nothing." Well, what if this is true? If this is the reality in which we live, then it truly matters what we are connecting people to when we bring them to faith in Jesus. It simply is not enough to attach them to the vine of our congregation or to the program we have set up. It is simply not enough to attract or attach them to our chosen method or plan. We absolutely must attach them to the Vine that gives life—eternal life.

Then what is the Vine? Let's go back to where it all started. "In the beginning was the Word, and the Word was with God, and the Word was God" (John 1:1). Jesus is the Word that became flesh, the very image of God, and Jesus called himself the Vine. Once a group of children were asked why Jesus was called the Word, and a little girl responded, "Because Jesus was all God wanted to say."

That is great truth from the mouth of a child!

With good intentions, we often try to protect people from Scripture. We keep them away from the boring parts and the controversial teachings. But, in reality, faith comes to life best in the early mornings when "every word that comes from the mouth of God" is laid out before us (Matt. 4:4). When we take time to read, question, and ponder the Word of God, we find life in it. When we pray through Scripture and fight to understand, we find peace and comprehension in an unbelievably complex world. We must never protect anyone from any part of God's Holy Word. In it is life—the fullness of life. In his book, *Peace with God*, Billy Graham said, "The very practice of reading in itself [the Bible] will have a purifying effect upon your mind and heart. Let nothing take the place of this daily exercise."[11]

Consider the following examples of powerful revival born out of a renewed focus on God's Word:

- Moses gave a send-off speech to the nation of Israel in Deuteronomy just before his death, and he emphasized the importance of this new Law in Chapter 11: "Fix these words of mine in your hearts and minds; tie them as symbols on your hands and bind them on your foreheads. Teach them to your children, talking about them when you sit at home and when you walk along the road, when you lie down and when you get up" (Deut. 11:18-19).

- At 26-years old, King Josiah had an entire nation turn back to God once his secretary, Saphan, read the Law that had been rediscovered

(2 Kings 22:8). One writer points out that the reading of God's Law "resulted in the most thoroughgoing religious reform Judah had ever seen."[12]

- Martin Luther and the Reformation happened because he was one of the only scholars left willing to read Scripture instead of commentary that the monks had relied on for so long. "But what Luther himself said many times was that the study of the Bible per se was simply unheard of in his early years as a monk. Of course there were no Bibles in pews and average laymen had almost no idea whatever of what it contained, nor even that it was a book."[13]

- William Wilberforce lived out the words of Psalm 119 that he often repeated, and he leaned on Scripture as his guide in the fight against the slave trade.

- Jesus constantly referred back to Scripture in his teachings, such as Matthew 4:4, 4:7, and 4:10.

There could be an entire book simply continuing this list. Our weakness is not in too much exposure to an outdated set of Scriptures. One of our primary weaknesses as modern Christians is an astonishing lack of exposure to the powerful and life-giving Word of God. "According to a recent news poll, eighty-eight percent of Americans own a Bible. The United States averages over four Bibles per household. But more than half of Americans open their Bibles less than four times a year."[14]

The lasting work of evangelism is to be found in connections. We must introduce people to Jesus (connection #1). We must introduce people to His Word—the Bible (connection #2). We must connect people to His followers—the Church (connection #3). When we connect people in these ways, we connect them to the Vine that is Jesus and is filled with the Holy Spirit. Once connected to the Vine, the lifeblood of the Holy Spirit can and does flow freely through the thoughts, habits, hurts, and hang-ups of the Jesus follower. In this connected reality, true life change takes place and true freedom is found. True Spirit-empowered, miraculous, evangelistic movements can begin and thrive.

This is what we are evangelizing people to.

This is where the power of the Methodist revivals came from.

This is where the power of all revivals comes from.

It has been said that the Church is the hope of the world. However, the truth is that the gospel, the Good News of Jesus and His love for all humanity, is the hope of the world. Our hope is in the love and forgiveness of Jesus, the life and culture-altering power of the Holy Spirit, and the sustaining and loving family of God.

The Church is simply the gospel's megaphone.

A megaphone multiplied by the countless millions who have found faith, hope, dignity, forgiveness, and power through Jesus, and are willing to let others know about Him.

This is evangelism.

This is our God-given command.

This can change the world.

So, for God's sake, let's go do our job.

ABOUT THE AUTHORS

MIKE HILSON is the Senior Pastor at NEWLIFE Church in La Plata, Maryland, and the author of several books and ministry resources. Since 1999, he has led his congregation into multiple church and video venues both locally and internationally. His wife, Tina, his sons, Robert, Stephen, and Joshua, and his daughters-in-law, Amanda and Alexa, join him in ministry. Books by Mike include *Napkin Theology, Speak Life, A Significant Impact for Christ, Heart of a Leader: Moses,* and a series of books called *Coffee with the Pastor.*

CURTIS HUNNICUTT is currently the Leadership Development Pastor at NEWLIFE Church in La Plata, Maryland. Formerly, he was Campus Pastor of NEWLIFE Calvert, which he planted and helped grow. He is also the founder of The Release Coaching Company, where he uses his passion to coach leaders. Curtis, his wife, Mathilda, and their two children are currently traveling around the country in a 5th Wheel planting house churches and working with pastors to help them effectively reach their communities. Curtis is the author of *The Millennial Manifesto.*

NOTES

PART 1

1. Barna, *Gen Z: The Culture, Beliefs and Motivations Shaping the Next Generation* (Ventura, CA: Barna Group, 2018), quoted in Barna, *Reviving Evangelism* (Barna Group, 2019), 21.

CHAPTER 1

1. *Merriam-Webster's Collegiate Dictionary*, 9th ed. (Philippines: Merriam-Webster Inc., 1991), 429.

2. *Merriam-Webster.*

3. Barna, *Reviving Evangelism* (Barna Group, 2019), 19.

4. David Kinnaman and Gabe Lyons, *Good Faith: Being a Christian When Society Thinks You're Irrelevant or Extreme* (Grand Rapids, MI: Baker Books, 2016), 42, quoted in Barna, *Reviving Evangelism* (Barna Group, 2019), 37.

5. Leon Trotsky, *Literature and Revolution* (New York: International Publishers Co., Inc., 1925), 255-256.

6. Palash Ghosh, "How Many People Did Joseph Stalin Kill?" International Business Times, IBTimes LLC, 2013, https://www.ibtimes.com/how-many-people-did-joseph-stalin-kill-1111789; Jung Chang and Jon Halliday, *Mao, The Unknown Story* (New York: Anchor Books, 2006), 613.

7. Robert Black and Keith Drury, *The Story of The Wesleyan Church* (Indianapolis, Indiana: Wesleyan Publishing House, 2018), 237.

8. Communication Team, "2018 TWC statistics reinforce need to fill the Gospel Gap," The Wesleyan Church, September 17, 2018, https://www.wesleyan.org/2018-twc-statistics-reinforce-need-to-fill-the-gospel-gap.

9. Black and Drury, *The Story of The Wesleyan Church*, 29-30.

CHAPTER 2

1. *Merriam-Webster's Collegiate Dictionary*, 9th ed. (Philippines: Merriam-Webster Inc., 1991), 627.

2. *Merriam-Webster*, 776.

3. Dr. Watson and Sue Black, eds., *North Carolina District Centennial*, 1879-1979 (North Carolina Colfax District, The Wesleyan Church, 1979).

4. Abraham Lincoln, "Gettysburg Address," Abraham Lincoln Online, Speeches & Writings, Gettysburg, Pennsylvania, November 19, 1863, http://www.abrahamlincolnonline.org/lincoln/speeches/gettysburg.htm.

5. Jung Chang and Jon Halliday, *Mao, The Unknown Story* (New York: Anchor Books, 2006), 613.

6. Palash Ghosh, "How Many People Did Joseph Stalin Kill?" International Business Times, IBTimes LLC, 2013, https://www.ibtimes.com/how-many-people-did-joseph-stalin-kill-1111789.

7. "Being Christian in Western Europe," Pew Research Center, Religion and Public Life, May 29, 2018, https://www.pewforum.org/2018/05/29/being-christian-in-western-europe.

8. The Wesleyan Church, 2018, https://www.wesleyan.org.

CHAPTER 3

1. *Merriam-Webster's Collegiate Dictionary*, 9th ed. (Philippines: Merriam-Webster Inc., 1991), 615.

2. *Merriam-Webster*, 259.

3. Robert Black and Keith Drury, *The Story of The Wesleyan Church* (Indianapolis, Indiana: Wesleyan Publishing House, 2018), 47 (hereafter cited in text as TWC).

4. Aldous Huxley, *Brave New World*, Harper Perennial Modern Classics ed. (New York: HarperCollins Publishers, 2006), 1 (hereafter cited in text as BNW).

CHAPTER 4

1. Friedrich Nietzsche, *The Gay Science* (New York: Vintage Books Edition, March 1974), 181.

2. *Merriam-Webster's Collegiate Dictionary*, 9th ed. (Philippines: Merriam-Webster Inc., 1991), 1222.

3. *Merriam-Webster*, 112.

4. Karl Marx and Friedrich Engels, *The Communist Manifesto* (New York: Pocket Books, Simon & Schuster Inc., 1964), 92.

5. Friedrich Nietzsche, *The Gay Science.*

6. Timothy J. Madigan, "Nietzsche & Schopenhauer On Compassion," Philosophy Now, 2000, https://philosophy now.org/issues/29/Nietzsche_and_Schopenhauer_ On_Compassion.

7. Eric Metaxas, *Amazing Grace* (New York: HarperCollins Publishers, 2008), 71.

8. "Is God Dead?" Time USA, LLC, April 8, 1966, 82, https://time.co/vault/issue/1966-04-08.

9. C.S. Lewis, *A Grief Observed* (New York: HarperCollins Publishers, 1994), 66.

CHAPTER 5

1. *Merriam-Webster's Collegiate Dictionary*, 9th ed. (Philippines: Merriam-Webster Inc., 1991), 246.

2. *Merriam-Webster*, 530.

3. Richard Delgado and Jean Stefancic, *Critical Race Theory*, 3rd ed. (New York: New York University Press, 2017), 9 (hereafter cited in text as CRT).

4. Helen Pluckrose and James Lindsay, *Cynical Theories* (Durham, North Carolina: Pitchstone Publishing, 2020), 237.

PART 2

1. Mark L. Gorveatte, *Lead Like Wesley* (Indianapolis, Indiana: Wesleyan Publishing House, 2016), 164.

CHAPTER 6

1. E.M. Bounds, *Power Through Prayer* (Middletown, DE, 2021), 1.

2. *Merriam-Webster's Collegiate Dictionary*, 9th ed. (Philippines: Merriam-Webster Inc., 1991), 994.

3. Eric Metaxas, *Amazing Grace* (New York: HarperCollins Publishers, 2008), 167 (hereafter cited in text as AG).

4. "Ralph Waldo Emerson Quotes," Good Reads, https://www.goodreads.com/quotes/8468-in-my-walks-every-man-i-meet-is-my-superior.

5. Alex Murashko, "Francis Chan at Exponential West: Church Planters Need to Set Aside 'a Lot of Strategies Out There' to Focus on Basic Gospel Message," The Christian Post, CP Church & Ministries, October 9, 2014, https://www.christianpost.com/news/francis-chan-at-exponential-west-church-planters-need-to-set-aside-a-lot-of-strategies-out-there-to-focus-on-basic-gospel-message.html.

CHAPTER 7

1. Nancy Flory, "Black Musician Talks Race With KKK Members — And Hundreds Have Quit the Klan Because of Him," The Stream, September 7, 2017, https://stream.org/black-musician-talks-race-with-kkk-members-and-hundreds-have-quit-the-klan-because-of-him.

2. *Merriam-Webster's Collegiate Dictionary*, 9th ed. (Philippines: Merriam-Webster Inc., 1991), 398.

3. Daryl Davis, Lyrad Productions, 2021, https://www.daryldavis.com.

4. Nancy Flory, "Black Musician Talks Race With KKK Members."

5. Matt Ornstein, Director, "Accidental Courtesy: Daryl Davis, Race & America," Amazon Prime Video, 14:04, 2016, https://www.amazon.com/Accidental-Courtesy-Daryl-Davis-America/dp/B07Z198CBP.

6. Ryan Holiday, *Ego is the Enemy* (New York: Penguin Random House LLC, 2016), 175.

7. The Veritas Forum, "Who Lights the Way for Jesus? | Daryl Davis," YouTube Video, 2:12, August 19, 2020, https://www.youtube.com/watch?v=Ygw02KbKZmo.

CHAPTER 8

1. Henry & Richard Blackaby, *Spiritual Leadership* (Nashville, Tennessee: Broadman & Holman Publishers, 2001), 100.

2. *Merriam-Webster's Collegiate Dictionary*, 9th ed. (Philippines: Merriam-Webster Inc., 1991), 980.

3. Oswald Chambers, *My Utmost For His Highest*, The Classic ed. (Uhrichsville, Ohio: Barbour & Company, Inc., 1963), 306.

CHAPTER 9

1. Emile Zola, quoted in Ryan Holiday, *Ego is the Enemy* (New York: Penguin Random House LLC, 2016), 182.

2. *Merriam-Webster's Collegiate Dictionary*, 9th ed. (Philippines: Merriam-Webster Inc., 1991), 1010.

3. "Wesley, the Moravian hymnwriter," Organists Do It With Pedals, October 29, 2015, https://organistsdoit withpedals.wordpress.com/2015/10/29/wesley-the-moravian-hymnwriter/#:~:text=When%20asked%20at %20the%20town,that%20was%20in%20Christ%20and.

4. *The Works of John Wesley*, 3rd ed., Complete and Unabridged, vol. 1, Journals from October 14, 1735 to November 29, 1745 (Grand Rapids, Michigan: Baker Book House Company, 1984), 103.

5. Robert Tombs, *The English and Their History* (New York: Vintage Books, A Division of Penguin Random House LLC, 2014), 289.

6. The Editors of Encyclopaedia Britannica, "Reign of Terror," Britannica, https://www.britannica.com/event/ Reign-of-Terror.

7. Robert Tombs, *The English and Their History*, 364-365.

8. Christopher Ion, "The Prayer Meeting That Saved England," Christian Heritage Fellowship, December 26, 2020, https://christianheritagefellowship.com/ prayer-meeting-that-saved-england.

9. Martin Luther, "Martin Luther's Definition of Faith," Ligonier Ministries, https://www.ligonier.org/learn/ articles/martin-luthers-definition-faith.

10. "John Wesley: The Man Who Saved England," YouTube Video, 23:02, May 24, 2019, https://www.youtube.com/watch?v=UwjdD_JbOok.

11. Billy Graham, *Peace with God* (Nashville, Tennessee: W Publishing Group, An imprint of Thomas Nelson, 1984), 216.

12. Philip Yancey and Tim Stafford, *NIV Student Bible* (Grand Rapids, Michigan: Zondervan, 2011), 445.

13. Eric Metaxas, *Martin Luther* (New York: Viking, An Imprint of Penguin Random House LLC, 2017), 52.

14. David M. Patterson, "The Importance of Bible Based on Jesus' Perspective on Scripture," *Diligence: Journal of the Liberty University*, vol. 1, article 8 (September 2016): 1, https://digitalcommons.liberty.edu/cgi/viewcontent.cgi?article=1009&context=djrc.